D0004568

ONE
DEGREE
REVOLUTION

ONE
DEGREE
REVOLUTION

How the Wisdom of Yoga Inspires
Small Shifts That Lead
to Big Changes

Coby Kozlowski

ST. MARTIN'S
ESSENTIALS
NEW YORK

First published in the United States by St. Martin's Essentials, an imprint of
St. Martin's Publishing Group

ONE DEGREE REVOLUTION. Copyright © 2019 by Coby Kozlowski. All rights reserved.
Printed in the United States of America. For information, address
St. Martin's Publishing Group, 120 Broadway, New York, NY 10271.

www.stmartins.com

Excerpt from "The Radiance Sutras" © 2014 Lorin Roche used with permission
from the publisher, Sounds True, Inc.

The Library of Congress Cataloging-in-Publication Data is available upon request.

ISBN 978-1-250-20175-1 (hardcover)
ISBN 978-1-250-20175-1 (ebook)

eISBN 9781250201751

Our books may be purchased in bulk for promotional, educational, or business use.
Please contact your local bookseller or the Macmillan Corporate and Premium
Sales Department at 1-800-221-7945, extension 5442, or by email at
MacmillanSpecialMarkets@macmillan.com.

First Edition: January 2020

10 9 8 7 6 5 4 3 2 1

For my daughter, Bowie

Contents

Acknowledgments

To all wisdom keepers who have walked a path of yoga before me, to my teachers and those who have studied with me, those who have assisted and supported me, and everyone who has taught me about love, truth, integrity, and freedom, I thank you.

I would like to thank my parents, William Kozlowski and Sheila Kozlowski, for being my first teachers and teaching me the power of generosity, kindness, resourcefulness, and unconditional love; my two older brothers whom I've always admired, Michael Kozlowski and Eric Kozlowski; and my cousin Kim Cassie who I've always thought of as the sister I wish I had. My loving sister-in-law Shannen Kozlowski, niece Kaili Kozlowski, and nephew Michael Kozlowski, remind me of the importance of family. Steven Leonard—thank you for riding the waves with me and being by my side as a truly incredible co-parent and partner. And to the Leonard family and the rest of my wonderful family—thank you.

Thank you to my friends and mentors who have opened my eyes to a greater truth and inspired, encouraged, and supported me. Thank you for *seeing* me, loving me, challenging me, calling me to a deeper level of integrity, cracking my heart open, and reminding me of the power of joy, wonder, and laughter: thank you Lorin Roche, Katie Brauer, Holly McCormack, Patrick Ryan, Lonny Jarrett, Sue Pentland, and Tory Smith. And a special thank-you to Danny Arguetty—thank you for being my teacher, my best friend, and my chosen family. I am beyond grateful for your love, brilliance, support, wisdom, and humor every step of the way. I truly could not have taken this journey without you.

I would also like to thank my publishing team who made this all possible: Pam Liflander—wow, thank you—there is no way I could ever thank you enough for helping me put my words on these pages. Thank you for your incredible talent, thoughtfulness, and patience. You are a true gift. Gareth Esersky at the Carol Mann Agency, thank you for making magic happen. Daniela Rapp and everyone at St. Martin's, thank you for believing in me and my work.

The faculty and staff at Kripalu Center for Yoga & Health, Esalen Institute, *Yoga Journal*, *Mantra Wellness* magazine, and all of the conferences, festivals, universities, magazines, and podcasts that have supported my work and my workshop, Quarter-Life Calling: Creating an Extraordinary Life in your 20s, which this book was originally based on.

And thank you to Jordan Grinstein for not taking notes during my workshop and patiently waiting for me to write this book.

Introduction

Imagine for a moment that we're all on a boat. Even though we've set a course for a particular destination, what would happen if we changed that course just one degree? How far from our original trajectory would we be in one year? Five years? Ten years? Twenty years? Thirty years? Fifty years? Well, you would end up in a totally different place.

What if I told you that you can shift the course of your life entirely by this same proverbial one degree—making a small course shift in one area of your life, or many? Over time, these small shifts will lead to big changes. The question is, where do you start? What do you need to investigate to find where you can make these small shifts?

This level of inquiry is the basis for what I call a one degree revolution; the starting point at which you can make small shifts to the way you are living that can lead to profound changes. I'm not asking you to do a complete transformation of every aspect of your life. Instead you'll see that by looking at your actions and intentions, you may discover something new about yourself and how you function in this world.

So where do we begin? For me, the teachings of yoga, and its applications to the modern world, offer the most meaningful, powerful, and impactful lessons. And I'm not talking about the yoga you might be doing on the mat. That's why this is not a yoga book, yet it is.

When people learn that I lead yoga workshops and train yoga teachers at some of the most established wellness centers, conferences, and festivals across the globe, most assume that means I'm leading downward-facing dog or some other *asana*, or posture, most of the day. I do believe the physical practice is a great doorway into this beautiful world of yoga, and the *asanas* can be beneficial to supporting and enhancing the way you feel about your entire being. Yet that's not the version of yoga I'm offering you in this book. It is not what I mean to convey when I tell people I'm a contemporary yoga and meditation educator, or how my life has been profoundly influenced by yoga.

I didn't realize the complexity and depth that yoga had to offer until I was badly injured in college. I had already been *doing* yoga for a few years. In fact, I took my first yoga class when I was seventeen. I have always been an athlete: in high school and college I was a marathon runner, triathlete, and a competitive swimmer. I defined myself by how my body performed. Yet I was also a *thinker*—often contemplating the meaning of life. To my seventeen-year-old brain, yoga sounded like the perfect mix.

I was intrigued by the mind-body connection, and fascinated by the physical practice. So I got on the mat, and much to my surprise I was truly disappointed: the first class just bored me. I didn't feel relaxed, peaceful, or in tune with my body. I don't know why I kept going, but I did. Eventually, my seventeen-year-old self learned to appreciate the strength, stability, fluidity, and introspection within the postures. I liked challenging myself both physically and mentally, whether it was the intensity of doing handstands and arm balances, learning to understand why postures that seemed easy were actually advanced, or fully letting go during relaxation and letting myself simply be.

One day, a few years after that first yoga class, my life changed in an instant. I was seriously injured in college playing Ultimate Frisbee. At the time I thought this was no big deal; I had taken a hard fall, and was supposed to have a routine ACL reconstruction on my knee. Yet for the next six years I was on and off crutches, and I ended up having nine surgeries. After the first surgery there were complications. I also had an allergic reaction to the anesthesia, which impacted both my healing and my vision. I ended up bedridden for three months: my life as I knew it was put on hold. I couldn't move, I couldn't see clearly, and I couldn't do what most other twenty-year-olds were doing. Instead, I was back at my parents' house, literally stuck in a bed in the middle of their living room.

Until then I had defined myself as both an athlete and a thinker. I was competitive, assertive, contemplative, and curious. I moved fast, I talked fast; I did just about everything fast. Now that I no longer could use my body in the same way, and with so much time on my hands, I began to go inward and think even more. I wondered a lot about who I was going to be if I couldn't use my physical body in the same way. Who am I really? Why am I here? How do I want to live? What happens when I die?

Within a few months my eyesight returned to normal, yet I was still stuck recovering in bed. Ruminating on these thoughts steered me toward investigating the other aspects of yoga, the teachings beyond the physical practice. Yoga turned out to be so much more than what I could do with my body. In fact, the yoga I had been practicing on the mat was just the beginning. Understanding and exploring the philosophy opened up a completely new way to see the world and the relationship I could have with it. I was being initiated into a path of *living* yoga, not just *doing* yoga.

As I looked for new or different ways to heal my physical body, I continued to deepen my inquiry with all aspects of yoga. I began to study as many different perspectives of the tradition as well as our innate human potential. I started combining the ancient teachings of yoga with studies in Ayurveda—the traditional Indian system of medicine often known as the sister science to yoga. I also studied more "Western" ideas like coaching, transformative leadership, positive psychology, expressive arts, and dance. Each of these studies challenged me, encouraged me, and helped me evolve into a different version of myself.

Yoga has provided me insights and opened up new inquiries that I was insatiably curious to unravel, and you might be as well: How can I best be with life? How can the teachings direct me to see the most aligned choices, let go of past hurts, and make meaningful connections? How can I be with all of my feelings, from sadness, grief, and sorrow, to ecstasy, joy, and bliss, and everything in between? How can I learn to be with both the highs and the lows that are part of everyday living? And what are the most skillful ways I can savor—appreciate, cherish, and fully experience—the life that has been bestowed upon me before it's over? As I came to a deeper understanding of these questions, I began to look at my habits, my wounds, my stories, and my beliefs, and saw that life was quietly offering me endless possibilities if only I could learn to let go and trust it. And once I embraced this way of living, I was able to feel a greater sense of ease and navigate the uncertainties of life more freely and lovingly.

Today, twenty-plus years into my journey, I consider myself a contemporary yoga and meditation educator, and I am passionate about sharing these concepts with others, like you. My hope is that you can use my present-day, practical perspective of yoga to find more meaning and authenticity in your own life.

Throughout this book, you will be introduced to ancient yoga philosophies that are adapted for our modern lives. These teachings have been selected to guide you to better know yourself and support you to be more adept in this world. I'm not taking you on a monk's path, or showing you how to transcend the earthly experience. Instead, I'll share what I've learned (up to this point, because there is *always* more to learn) and offer you ways to deeply engage with the life you have right now. Some of these lessons might feel like a big wake-up call to make a change, or a gentle reminder of what you already knew about yourself, or a quiet whisper that's trying to get your attention.

So welcome to your journey into living yoga, which is my yoga offering to you. My aim is to support you to savor the gift of life more fully, and I'm honored you are here.

Become a Wave Rider

There are many different styles and philosophies of yoga, and what I offer in this book might be a little different than what you've heard about yoga, or even yoga philosophy. This is not a book on the history of yoga, and I'm not here to guarantee happiness or lifelong fulfillment. Instead, we're going to take a journey together so that you can figure out, for yourself, how living yoga might support your ability to remember your truth, connect with what you deeply care about, and better ride life's ups and downs, or what I call the waves of life.

We all know that life is brief, yet more often than not, we don't treat it as a rare, precious, and beautiful experience. Instead, we can get swept away in the to-dos of life and lose sight of the power we inherently have to fully participate and engage. And consequently too many people feel dissatisfied with their lives. Some are questioning decisions they've made, or feel like they've been sucked into a riptide, swept away with the flow, and don't know where to look for answers. Others are deeply disconnected, lonely, anxious, depressed, angry, and irritated. Some are longing to find their purpose, or a deep and intimate connection with life, yet feel that they only exist on the surface of their experience, jumping from one thing to the next without taking the time to see what is working for them and what isn't.

I know so many people who feel like they are drowning because life seems too fast, too turbulent. The rapid pace of the world and its relentless stimulation can make it difficult to stop and listen to our inner wisdom, the quiet voice within. This is especially true because most of us haven't been taught how to trust our intuition or inner knowing. Without this knowledge, we can feel adrift, tired, scattered, confused, and craving hope, direction, realness, and inspiration.

The truth is, we can't predict how our lives will go, or how rough or calm the ocean will be. Yet imagine how differently you might feel if you could learn to approach what the world throws at you with grace? My hope is that the lessons in this book will help you to learn how to be with the waves, and how to ride them skillfully.

Let's Get on the Boat: Small Shifts Lead to Big Changes

I've gone through big shifts, like changing careers or moving across the country. And then I've made other very small shifts, like finding the value in taking a deep breath so that I can pause before I speak.

While the small shifts may not seem as dramatic as the big ones, they have actually had an equal and sometimes bigger impact on my life, because they create a habit that enriches and generates more ease in my daily life.

This one degree revolution is a path of self-discovery that is based on putting yourself into a series of personal inquiries within the philosophical framework of yoga. Some might offer you inspiration to make a one degree shift. Some offer the ability to reflect on your past, while others focus on the present. Others are meant to encourage you to take a particular action. Each one may provide a new way of challenging your beliefs or taking a skillful action step—more doing than learning from an "expert." That's intentional, because I know that I do not have the answers you may be seeking. Nobody can live your life for you or tell you what is the best way for you to act, feel, or think. However, I can provide questions, inquiries, and experiments that you can use to explore the ways you are currently riding the waves so that you can unveil your personal truths. When you put yourself in your own inquiries and experiments, welcome vulnerability, and gather new data, you open the door to possibility and change.

The skillful actions you choose can be reflected in every area of your life. If you're continually checking in with yourself and noticing what makes you feel most alive, that will affect your habits around food, sleep, and exercise; your relationships and communication with others; the way you tend to the space you live in; really just about everything. Remember, yoga is a lifelong practice. With every action we're coming home to the unique experience of being ourselves. We can move in that direction while staying open to the process of refinement and continual learning. However, in order to take that first step toward skillful action you must be willing first to show up and put yourself in the experiment.

Where do you want to thrive more? Maybe it's your career,

personal development, your finances, or your romantic life. What has been trying to get your attention—that maybe you have been ignoring? What small shift are you being called to make that could shift you in a new direction?

Each of the following chapters includes many one degree shift inquiries that are inspired by different yogic teachings. Think of them like rituals, or sacred ceremonies, rather than just something you're supposed to do. Whatever you want to work through, or whatever aspect of your life is signaling for attention, will most likely show itself. Certain inquiries might make you feel more grounded, more clear, more connected. Others might point at the obstacles that are holding you back, which might show up as resistance, uncertainty, or confusion.

You do not have to do all of the inquiries at once, or in order, or at all. They are simply an offering or an invitation for you to dive into self-exploration. No one can do the work for you, and it's up to you to accept or decline these invitations. My suggestion is to read the book from beginning to end, and see which inquiries resonate. I've found the ones that don't are usually the ones you might want to look at first. Have you ever heard the saying, *What you resist persists?* Sometimes our blind spot, the thing about ourselves we can't see, is actually the one thing that can help us the most, if we pay attention to it.

Living yoga is a path of transformation, because one of the few guarantees of life is that things will change. In order to thrive, you are invited to participate in the co-creation of the life you truly want. As you start working with these inquiries you will cultivate a stronger sense of resilience to ride the waves of life, so ultimately you can appreciate as many moments in life as possible.

In Chapter 1, Living Yoga, you'll learn more about my philosophy of living yoga, and the traditional themes and teachings it is based on. While I have been in the yoga world for many years and have studied various streams of philosophy, I don't claim to be a scholar of this ancient tradition. I recognize that many of these ideas and concepts originated from a culture outside of my own and my intent is not to appropriate or disrespect these origins. While these concepts will always have ties to the past, it is their iteration and evolution in the here and now that interests me most and motivates me to share my version of how to participate in the practice of yoga, and how it can influence the way we look at ourselves, and the world.

Chapter 2, Sitting in the Fire, offers specific inquiries and lessons that show how to better handle the discomfort that often comes with growth and change. When life gets challenging, learning to stay in the heat instead of jumping ship can lead to a powerful transformation. Yoga teaches us how to get comfortable being uncomfortable, and how discerning between *sensation* and *pain* can lead to growth.

In Chapter 3, Dare to Be Your Authentic Self, you will begin the process of discovering a new level of personal authenticity: what is real and true for you. One of the ways that we live yoga is learning to align the physical body with the breath body, the mental body, the witness, and the bliss body. When this happens, you are more likely to appreciate and live as your most aligned self, or what I call your authentic self.

Chapter 4, Accountability and Integrity explores the yoga of accountability: Patton Sarley, the former CEO of the Kripalu Center for Yoga & Health, also often known by his yoga name of Dinabandhu, defines yoga as the practice of tolerating the consequences of being ourselves. How do we learn to balance the fact that we're always evolving, yet honor that there is a perfection just in being who we already are? Yoga teaches that we're always evolving into a different perfection. The inquiries in this chapter will invite you to both trust where you're at and where you're going, and show why it's helpful to clean up any messes you might have made along the way.

Chapter 5, Your Sacred Community, reminds us that we each are a part of a sacred community and that no matter how difficult life becomes, we're never riding the waves alone. Finding community is a key to living our lives in the most fulfilling way possible.

Chapter 6, Instinctive Meditation, explores a different approach to meditation, a practice that is meant for a *householder*, the name of a yoga practitioner that lives in the world (as opposed to a monk). Instinctive meditation is the inward inquiry that will support you in embracing the movement of life so that you can have a more intimate relationship with it, and listen to your inner voice even more deeply.

Chapter 7, The Power of Pause, explains the value of taking a pause. This practice can empower us as we learn that even in the fullness of life we can step back for just a moment. It provides inquiries that focus on identifying the sweetness and beauty already present in our lives, and how our vital life force of breath can help identify and create the metaphorical space for consciously connecting our feelings, thoughts, and our actions.

Chapter 8, Rewriting Your Story, explores the many ways we can challenge long-held beliefs that may not be serving us. I like to refer to this as composting: how we can take the shit in our lives and turn it into something useful. When we can rewrite the unhelpful or misinformed beliefs that motivate so many of our decisions, we can create a more supportive reality for ourselves by crafting a new narrative.

Chapter 9, Trust Life, helps us learn to trust life so that we can let go of what we cannot control, and ultimately surrender by tapping into the intelligence of nature which weaves itself through every facet of life. These inquiries can help us trust our own resourcefulness and the abundance present at all levels of existence.

In chapter 10, Callings, you'll begin to start listening for your calling—your life's purpose. While every chapter offers potential one degree shifts, here you'll be able to take the very first steps toward discovering what is trying to get your attention. And, you will explore how you can make small shifts for the sake of the greater collective, our global consciousness. You don't need to save the world to save the world. By saying yes to your one degree shifts, you can help create positive change beyond your individual path.

Chapter 11, Begin Again, teaches that there's always another chance for a fresh start, as long as we're still in the game. Sometimes our small shifts lead to the changes we anticipate, and sometimes not. No matter what unfolds, or how the experiment goes, yoga reminds us that with each breath comes a new opportunity: we can always begin again.

Let's begin together on this living yoga journey and start your one degree revolution.

Get on the boat.
Ride the waves.
Trust life.
Savor life.
Live in wonder.

Living Yoga

Yoga is saying yes *to this moment. Because this is
the moment to begin.
Yoga is saying* yes *to engaging. Because participating
in this moment will impact your future.
Yoga is saying* yes *to curiosity. Because staying open to this
moment can broaden your understanding of the past.
Yoga is a paradox. It is will. It is surrender. It is black,
and white, and every color in between.
Yoga is something to experience. It is love.
Yoga is becoming intimate with all of life. Because yoga is life.*

So what is yoga anyway, if it isn't just about the physical postures? To define yoga is, in a sense, to define life. For some it's a very personal physical practice. For others it's a spiritual practice. For some it's everything in between.

If you ask one hundred yoga teachers for a full definition of yoga you'll probably get one hundred different answers. For me, the definition of yoga begins with its root. The Sanskrit dictionary defines *yuj*, which is the root word for yoga, as "to yoke, to harness, or to come together." A contemporary interpretation of this root word places yoga as "the skillful participation and engagement with the movement of life": an opportunity to find a deeper and more intimate connection with everything we experience, and exploring these connections in an honest and responsible way. Yoga is a path of transformation. This book is meant to provide suggestions for a multitude of ways that you can more skillfully participate and engage with life.

Yoga is not about escaping the everyday aspects of life, or putting aside your problems for an hour while you stretch. It is not about transcending to a higher state or disassociating from the real world. Instead, yoga allows us to fall in love with all of life by trusting the possibilities put before us, and learning how to rides the waves—the ups and downs we are faced with every day—with skill and grace. It teaches us to deeply listen and to trust the inner voice that guides us into discovering who we really are, and to see life clearly, as Patton Sarley says, "beyond the fear, fantasy, and distortions"; the misperceptions of circumstances. Imagine you are at a carnival and you're in the fun house of mirrors. Each time you look in a mirror you see your face differently: sometimes it's long, sometimes it's wide, but each time you know what you see isn't real. Yet many people go through their life looking through this distorted lens and unknowingly create limits, fears, fantasies, and unnecessary suffering for themselves.

For instance, after your first heartbreak, you might have created the distortion that you are not lovable. You may have repeatedly told yourself this "fact," and then you reinforced it by collecting data that supports your idea, like whenever someone doesn't text back or return phone calls. You've now created a false belief that the data is proving your idea, and even if it isn't true, you continue to see the world through this lens.

One of the intentions of yoga is to help you recognize when you are distorting what's really happening when you stay in the fun house. Once you realize that, the power comes from understanding you have a choice to leave the fun house, and then you will be able to see your life with fresh, clear eyes.

Each of us is encouraged to walk our own path, and to trust the teacher that lives within. To live yoga is to learn to listen to this inner teacher that is guiding us home to our truest self. Though there is no "right way" to begin this journey, you can start by exploring some of the tradition's overarching teachings, and see how they can support this journey.

A Word About Sanskrit

Sanskrit is an ancient language from India dating back almost 3,500 years. It is the language of yoga, which was primarily taught through oral repetition. It is a language built around the root of a word, and consequently, many words can be interpreted differently.

I am not a Sanskrit scholar, yet I use Sanskrit words and their definitions. I have a deep appreciation for the language, and want to bridge the lessons in this book and the ancient tradition of yoga, adapted for today. I love learning and sharing this language, as each word feels like a poem that describes an experience, place, or feeling in a way that an English translation can't always match.

Yoga Is Traditional

As yoga developed over thousands of years, four paths emerged as foundational and remain relevant today. Each path can be used as a resource for contemplation and to teach us skillful engagement. They also provide great starting points for diving into the inquiries for your own one degree revolution. Even though they may seem different, at their core they are complementary.

Most people are introduced to yoga through the physical practice. This is one of the four paths, known as *hatha yoga*. Hatha yoga allows us to use the body as a sacred doorway that can lead to increased self-awareness and curiosity.

Traditional hatha yoga is different than the yoga most commonly taught today. In the past, the postures were less about the way the physical body could perform and more about the ways we could purify the body and build mental strength to prepare for meditation. The postures today can be tools to recalibrate, heal, energize, and reconnect to the body, while also building mental strength. When you're holding a pose, it invites you to check in and notice different parts of your body and the sensations that are created. Are your feet firmly planted on the ground? What do you notice in your back? Your arms? What do you notice with your breath? What is the relationship between your body, breath, and mind?

Hatha yoga also incorporates taking care of your physical body—the vehicle that allows you to enjoy the human experience—and when practiced in a compassionate way, it can rejuvenate and rebalance. As the physical body opens and you breathe more deeply and consciously, it can result in increased vitality, which can allow you to more fully participate in life.

While this book doesn't focus on hatha yoga, it is an excellent way into the yoga experience. It's just not the only way.

Bhakti yoga is the practice of heart-centered dedication and devotion. Traditionally, this path focused on devoting yourself to a particular god or goddess. Bhakti teachings include having compassion for all, taking time to pray, and the ritual chanting to a god/goddess or some divine source by reciting repetitive sounds or mantras. Today we can think of bhakti in broader terms as devoting ourselves to what we value most. It might be a dedication to your life's purpose or calling, personal growth, family, the environment, or community.

Later in the book we will explore inquiries that will help you think more deeply about your purpose or calling, which can be a pursuit you choose to devote yourself to that is uplifting to yourself and/or the world, even in the smallest way. Once you identify your calling, the next step is deciding how to take action to achieve it. Bhakti yoga teaches that it can be more effective when it comes from a place of love, kindness, and compassion.

Karma yoga is traditionally the yoga of action, a "call to service" for the good of humankind. As with many words in Sanskrit there are multiple definitions of karma. When most people hear the word "karma" they think of the idea of what goes around comes around, or cause and effect. Yet in this case, karma yoga means something different: it invites us to step forward and do meaningful work in the world without the attachment to immediate reward or even recognition. And while we are not attached to a particular reward, there is often an insight or wisdom that shows up as we do this work. Ultimately this wisdom can help you remain dedicated to your calling for the sake of creating something different, something worthwhile, or something of value.

We can also think of karma yoga as self-full service: How do I become who I really am—and live in alignment with my most empowered, fullest self? What inner work do I need to do so I can be of service to others? Yoga teaches that what each of us offers to the

world has an impact, and that we are weaving and looming something together, our human experience—which has a greater impact on the world at large—the animals, the plants, the planet, the
oceans. We are called to take responsibility for what we are creating together—and most of us would agree—that although there is so
much beauty in the world, there's also a lot of pain. This leads me to
believe that there has to be another way to live than how we are living
now, and each one of us can contribute by making a shift. Part of the
complexity of living yoga is recognizing the perfection that is here in
this moment, and that there is also another future perfection that we
can evolve into.

Lastly, *jnana yoga* is the path of knowledge and connecting to the
wisdom of yoga: what we deem as useful and what will support us to
thrive on our path. Traditionally, knowledge was gained through the
study of the scriptures. Today we can expand this to reading books
that spark awareness or creativity, immersing ourselves in art, being
in nature, observing oneself, and learning about our relationships
with others. My hope is that through the inquiries in this book you
will be able to access this path of knowledge. You are then invited to
embody what you learn through practice and dedication. I believe
that wisdom comes from doing the inner work, and helps us be of
service to ourselves and ultimately to others, the community or the
larger global family. The way to reveal your greatest truth and understand the power of your own one degree revolution is by taking
on these inquiries. That's why the definition of yoga as skillfully
participating and engaging with life is so powerful. It's not simply
studying the menu of life, it's the act of tasting the food.

Of these four traditional paths, this book focuses most on karma
yoga, jnana yoga, and bhakti yoga. Each of these inspires how we
live yoga—not just do yoga.

Yoga Is Contemporary

While yoga is traditional, there's a benefit in bringing these teachings to meet the needs of the world we're living in today. How do we honor tradition and also recognize that we live in a different world and a different time?

In my practical view, I don't subscribe to just one school of yoga thought. This book is an invitation to explore many different traditions of yoga that offer different perspectives and tools that I believe can be helpful for living in our contemporary world. In some ways, this book is exploring many different gateways into living yoga, while you dive deep into getting to know yourself more intimately.

Yoga Is a Technology

You can also think of yoga as a technology: the application of knowledge to a practical purpose. In this case, the teachings of yoga contain knowledge that if implemented can lead to a more fulfilling life. And of course, within the application of yoga are separate technologies that are meant to support your path. These are the inquiries you will be placing yourself in.

Yoga teaches that a more fulfilling life includes the following four aims, which are called the *purushartas*:

Kama: The desires and pleasures of life. Kama is about having a healthy relationship with your desires. From this perspective of yoga, desires are neither bad nor wrong; it's the perspective you have and the way you engage with your desires that may need some fine-tuning to generate an optimal relationship.

Artha: Inner and outer prosperity. The aim is to both provide for yourself and have the satisfying feeling of abundance that comes from within.

Moksha: The pursuit and sense of liberation and internal freedom. It is the realization that you do not need to be a victim to your circumstances.

Dharma: Duty or purpose. Dharma helps answer the questions of why we are here on this planet. It begs the questions: What is it that you want to do? How do you want to express yourself within your relationships, your work, and your life purpose?

No one of these four aims is more important than the others. In fact, these four aims are always interwoven, working together to support your life's path. You might even start to feel like something's off when one of these four aims is not being fulfilled. For instance, if you feel like you are unable to source happiness from the inside or you don't have a sense of prosperity or worth, that can create disappointment or even anxiousness. The key is learning how to navigate and cultivate a healthy relationship with these four aims at any given time.

The inquiries are intended to help you discover what is real and true for you, what has heart and meaning for you, and how you want to be in a relationship with these four aims. For instance, you will be invited to become more honest about what you really desire, what true prosperity means for you, what freedom means for you, and what your purpose is. And as we continue to journey and blossom into the next version of ourselves, we can come back and begin the experiments again. What's fulfilling now? What are my desires now? What does prosperity mean to me now? What does freedom mean to me now? What is my purpose now?

Activating Your Witness Consciousness

One of the benefits of yoga is the practice of tapping into your witness consciousness: the ability for self-observation with compassion and discernment. The inquiries in this book aim to support you in strengthening this skill. As you begin to notice the beliefs that keep you from experiencing a greater sense of truth, or your most aligned self, or when you can see the many ways you resist fully embracing the beautiful gift of life, or the judgments you've made that no longer serve (the harsh and irrational ones), you can move toward making the necessary and potent small shifts that create lasting change.

Swami Kripalu, a yoga teacher who inspired the teachings of Kripalu yoga, has been credited in saying, "The highest form of spiritual practice is self-observation without judgment." I think there is value in self-judgment, as in discernment. I would offer that a more contemporary take on this quote could be, "The highest form of spiritual practice is self-observation with self-compassion."

Yoga Is an Inquiry

Beyond the historical perspective, yoga remains a powerful and compelling way to look at your life, think about change, and see the small shifts you can make so that you can skillfully engage. It supports this process by posing inquiries that allow you to be able to come closer to answering the questions, Who am I? Why am I here? How do I want to live? These questions point to the choices you make each day and operate on many levels, ranging from what do I want to eat, to who do I want to spend time with, to how can I be of service to others?

Regardless of your current relationship with yoga—whether you've started on a hatha yoga path or are coming to these teachings for the very first time—yoga is welcoming, and you can begin living yoga right now. The lessons and inquiries in this book are meant to meet you exactly where you are at, in whatever wave you are experiencing. The first step is simply to show up. From there the path opens in countless ways that invite you to participate. The following qualities are some broad and general guidelines for how to live yoga. They are the starting points to keep in mind as you dive into the inquiries. As you go through this book, just for now, toss aside what you think you already know about yourself, life, and yoga, and dare to embrace the wild unknown: the infinite possibilities awaiting you. If you are willing to believe that yoga is an inquiry, you can open up to the great adventure awaiting you.

As much as I value having a deep reverence for life and doing the work to begin your one degree revolution, I also think there's value in finding a balance between putting in the effort and stepping back to simply be and savor. Everything doesn't have to feel like you're carrying the weight of the world on your shoulders, and you don't always have to be so hard on yourself. When life begins to feel like a burden, it's easy to forget to focus on what is going well in our day-to-day, or the sweetness of the moments before us, or the magic that exists all around us.

As you work through the inquiries, see where you can add some lightness to your approach. The inquiries you are about to explore can be the keys to a playful journey if you approach them with wonder. This process of stepping into living yoga may have moments that feel challenging while other times it will be more fun and joyful. The opportunity is to see if you can stay open to everything that shows up. The first step is saying yes to the journey and making the commitment to stay on the path, during both the joyful moments and the challenges. What will make the difference in your experience is how you choose to participate.

Another one of yoga's teachings is to hold a posture of *sthira*, or steadiness, and *sukha*, or ease. These teachings apply to both yoga postures on the mat, and the mind-set you hold while living yoga off the mat. What would steadiness and ease look like for you when life is flowing as well as when life gets challenging? Keep this posture in mind as you dive into the inquiries throughout this book.

Yoga Is Intimacy

Living yoga invites us to create intimate relationships and be in awe of our creativity, enthusiasm, and the pure delight of being alive. It asks us to look directly at our life as we are experiencing it, leaving nothing out. It means being so dedicated to experience life more fully that you are willing to dissolve who you think you are for the sake of who you really are. It allows you to connect with the tides of terror and joy, will and surrender, pain and pleasure. It allows you to befriend the ache in your heart and see this ache as sacred. It is another paradox that invites you to fully feel as you learn how to ride the waves—the ups and downs of life—with grace and an open heart and mind.

Yoga teaches the myth that it was a roar of joy that put everything in the universe into motion. Part of learning to be intimate with life is to be inundated with the essence of joy and learning to be curious with the terror. If we are open to having an intimate relationship with the deepest sense of truth—which means leaving nothing out and welcoming everything in—you will find that you can offer your heart to the vast mystery of life itself, gaining a deeper sense of compassion to everything and everyone around you.

Yoga Is Deep Listening

Yoga teaches the art of listening, which includes both internal listening and external listening. Many people wonder what life is all about, what it is made up of, what we are here to do, and who we are at our core. When we learn to deeply listen to our own heart's desires, we can be introduced to love, beauty, and a natural intoxication with life itself. Dr. Lorin Roche, author of *The Radiance Sutras*, teaches that when you deeply listen to the whispers of life, you can hear the calling to "enter into the vastness of the heart and give yourself to it with total abandon." When you deeply listen and learn to trust life, a feeling of being at home in the universe can wash over you. A feeling that you fully belong here.

Each inquiry in this book is intended to boost your ability to deeply listen to your inner voice and hear the messages that have been trying to get your attention. And in this process you will learn how to pay more attention to the world around you so that you can better be in a state of alignment where your words, actions, thoughts, body, mind, heart, breath, and witness consciousness are working together.

For instance, the idea of making even small shifts might feel like too much. There are so many places you could look at in your life and see that things are out of balance or not working. It might be a relationship, or work, your health, or spiritual growth. Even if these areas seem like separate silos, when you deeply listen, you will learn how every aspect of your life is intermingled.

The key is to be able to hear what's trying to get your attention. This is the real value of learning to listen so that we don't simply go through life reacting to every drama or wave and every negative thought that comes our way. Instead, when we listen more deeply we can stay curious, take a step back, and make more informed decisions.

Yoga Is Opening to the Mystery of Life

Yoga is like the scientific method. We start with a hypothesis—the inquiries—and then put ourselves in different experiments for the sake of reaching a conclusion. This perspective on yoga teaches that there's no such thing as certainty; there is at best a likely scenario. However, when we get curious, skillfully participate, and are open to uncertainty, we create a higher probability for our intended outcome. And if we don't achieve what we desired, we can relax into the mystery of what can show up instead.

Many people are uncomfortable being in the mystery of life— the existential questions of what's really going on around us, or what happens when we die—and have habits or strategies to try and fill the void of not knowing, so that they don't have to feel this uncertainty, fear, or anxiety. So we often choose a distraction: wasting time on our phones, eating mindlessly, spending time with people and not really being present, ignoring our feelings. Sometimes a moment of distraction can feel useful—it can be a pause or time to reset—but when it becomes dominant or habitual it can turn into a crime against wisdom: knowing deep down that some action or idea is not helpful, and doing it anyway. Some would call this behavior self-sabotaging. A crime against wisdom could be staying up too late when you know you would feel better getting more rest, or eating sugar when you know you feel more alive when you don't, or staying in a relationship that you know is unhealthy. We commit these crimes against wisdom because we often don't know what else to do; we can feel stuck in a riptide, not consciously thinking that we have choices, and don't know how to get out. Or, we desperately want to leave, but don't realize we have the tools to get us out of the current.

When we recognize these crimes against wisdom and choose a more affirming path, we can still encounter obstacles. For instance, whenever I am called to make some kind of one degree shift to help me live with greater alignment or to get me out of a riptide, often the first feeling I encounter is the obstacle of resistance. When resistance rears its head, I get extra curious about what is going on because my resistance is often a "gremlin" or self-sabotaging part of myself that doesn't want to let go of the habit or have to do the real work to evolve and get out of the riptide. Often when I feel a resistance I wonder, is this resistance appearing to protect me or is it holding me back? Then I remember that the path of yoga provides infinite inquiries and infinite experiments to support reaching a more fulfilling life. Resistance gives us an opportunity to trust, and most likely, when you are close to something that is calling you to evolve, shift, or let go, that resistance might make an appearance. Then, when I ask myself the questions, what is truer than my resistance? What am I prepared to do about it? I often find a pot of gold—a world of potential growth opportunities. And when I am willing to face this part of myself with gentleness and humility, I often come through to the other side being a more aligned version of myself.

So let's get curious. No matter what inquiry you are invited into, you are in charge of which ones to participate in and what ideas you take from them. The process might be a bit more easeful if you start by taking off your armor (resistance) and putting your weapons down (complaining, pointing the finger, being the victim).

ONE DEGREE SHIFT INQUIRY:
Recognizing Crimes Against Wisdom

Your first inquiry explores something most people grapple with: making decisions that don't always serve your best interest. Aside from the example I've given, see where else you are committing crimes against wisdom in your life:

- Make a list of the areas in your life where are you committing crimes against wisdom. For example, you might already know that you're in the habit of staying up too late.
- What is the impact of these crimes against wisdom? For example, you might feel exhausted during the day, or feel unfocused or inattentive.
- What is a one degree shift you could make that can lead to a healthier outcome? For example, a simple shift could be to make a commitment to go to bed by 10 p.m. and setting a reminder on your phone to help you stay accountable.
- What is the potential value of staying committed to making this shift even when it's easier to fall back into your old habit? For example, the potential value might be feeling more alive and refreshed, and having more energy.
- How might you or others benefit from its value? For example, you might be able to get more done, appreciate your day more, or be more present with others.

Yoga Is Embracing Desires

Yoga teaches that we can have a healthy relationship with desire and the pleasures of life. Desire is an evolutionary impulse that calls you to act, pursue, respond, and participate: it can get you to where you want to be, who you want to be, and how you want to live. In some yogic perspectives, everything that we experience originates from the energy of desire. Desire can cause great suffering when it leads to an insatiable hunger powered by greed, which can deplete your vitality and often ends up hurting others. Or, it can be the evolutionary impulse that moves us forward toward action, love, healing, or transformation. When your desires are connected with your *dharma*, or life purpose, being of service to yourself and the greater good of those around you, it can become fuel for living a vibrant existence. The intention is to be moved by desire without being overly attached to the outcome, and learning to be open to the changes life will inevitably bring.

Yoga Is Freedom

We are not always free to do whatever we want, or change our external circumstance, yet we can change our perspective on it. No one can take away the freedom of how we feel inside. One of the most radical and courageous acts of navigating life with more awareness is to access this inner freedom. That's why I say that freedom is an inside job: we don't need to be a victim to our circumstances. When we sense a feeling of being trapped or imprisoned, we can step back from the moment, and purposefully respond. In this way we can access our internal freedom and create a new perspective for the sake of making a one degree shift to get on a new path.

Yoga Is a Pulsation

Yoga invites us to celebrate the life force known as *prana*, and honor the sacred tremor or pulse of life known as *spanda*. This pulse infuses everything, and is always available. Because of this yoga reminds us to be open, because this pulse invites life to move, and to move us forward, and therefore can change in an instant.

Yoga is an inhalation and exhalation. It is a process of opening and closing, of birth and death. Yoga is paradoxical because it invites us to be here in this present moment, and allows us to hope for a future, and honor our past.

Yoga teaches that the universe is filled with dancing particles of energy, and we can align ourselves with this pulsation. Our heart pulses, our breath moves, and our mind can wander—which is a beautiful ability and not a problem to be solved. Life involves both forgetting and remembering who we really are and why we are here. And, when we realize that we are whole and complete just the way we are, and we are here to experience life, there comes a feeling of joy in this remembrance. This joy can be a source of inspiration for others when they forget.

We are all in this intricate, conscious process of life together; each of us is more than just our physical body. Honoring this pulsation, rather than beating ourselves up for when we forget the big picture, can become our ticket to freedom.

Yoga Is Consciousness

Yoga invites us into a deep inquiry about the essence of consciousness. I don't believe that anybody truly knows for sure what consciousness is. Yet to talk about it, we need to have a working definition to play with.

To me, there is a difference between being conscious—or aware—of something, and consciousness. The way I experience and define consciousness—though I can't say that this is the *only* or the *right* definition—is that it is everything that ever was, and was not, everything that is, and is not, and everything that will be and will never be. It is both the potential of something to come into form, and the manifestation of that potential. Consciousness is both the blank canvas and the masterpiece that gets created on it.

Yoga teaches that there are six different qualities of consciousness; the different ways that consciousness can be expressed. We can use each as a tool when the waves seem too big to navigate. We will explore each of these in more detail throughout the book:

Svatantrya: Freedom is our inherent birthright; where am I imprisoning myself, and how can I access inner freedom?

Purnatva: Everything is perfect and always evolving into a different perfection. The opportunity is to see the perfection in this moment, and then ask the question, How can I also be open to a skillful, different perfection that is always available?

Kula: The sacred community: where or when am I feeling like I have to do everything myself, and forgetting that I can ask for help from others?

Rahasya: There are aspects of life that are secreted, and there is always more to come. Where am I not trusting that there is something I'm not aware of in this moment, and that there is more that will be revealed to me?

Chit: There is an intelligence woven into the fabric of life itself. Where can I let go of trying to control the uncontrollable, and trust the intelligence of life?

Shri: There is an abundance in life. Where am I looking at life through the lens of scarcity?

Yoga Is the One Degree Revolution

The one degree revolution is a conscious pushing back against your status quo. You can begin creating a life that has meaning, purpose, and passion; you do not have to keep living a life that's making you unfulfilled, because yoga teaches that there is always more of life available for you.

Yoga reminds us that life consistently provides the opportunities to participate and engage. And every step, every moment, is precious. Don't worry about seeing the end of the road or how it will all unfold. Trust that each step along the way is a sacred part of your journey. When you're walking in the dark and have a flashlight to help you see, it usually can only shine its light ten feet or so ahead. You still need to walk carefully, one step at a time. This book can be like that flashlight that guides you, one step at a time, toward your next destination. The key is to stay open, curious, and connected along the way. And trust that no matter where you end up, you can always take another step, even if it's in a totally different direction than where you thought you were headed. Each decision weaves together. And so every step along your path is honorable and has great value, even though some steps may seem like huge leaps and others may seem like you have hardly moved.

The rest of the chapters are opportunities to dive more deeply into many of these concepts as well as other important aspects of what yoga "is." Each one is a separate invitation into your one degree revolution to discover the most affirming ways to savor life. Whenever I feel uncertain, unclear, or off, I check in with the teachings in each of these chapters, almost like a compass to see what small shifts I can make that can lead to big changes.

Yoga is a path to unveil what is true and real.
Yoga is becoming intimate with all of life.
Yoga is living in wonder.
Yoga is riding the waves.
Yoga is an art and science.
Yoga is authenticity.
Yoga is integrity.
Yoga is accountability.
Yoga is community.
Yoga is walking through the sacred fire.
Yoga is freedom within boundaries.
Yoga is holding on and letting go.
Yoga is savoring.
Yoga is learning to trust that life changes and to be
open to those changes.
Yoga is living your purpose.
Yoga is a path of transformation.
Yoga is a practice for life.

Sitting in the Fire

Where do you go when life gets hot?
When the windows are closed and the doors are locked?
Have the willingness to stay and sit in the fire
For the sake of what is on the other side.
When you walk through the flames with love and compassion,
face your fears and challenge your demons.
You give yourself the gift
of knowing how powerful you truly are.

Your one degree revolution welcomes the transformative power of *agni*, the element of fire, and all that it can symbolize. Agni refers to both the literal fire that provides heat and light, and the internal fire we carry. A person who chooses to walk a path of yoga and learns to use the transformative power of fire often emits a glow, a radiance and luminosity of health and vitality.

We need fire in order to digest, or to reap the full benefits of, our food, emotions, and experiences. It is the catalyst that can create change, and our ability to be with fire is necessary for making a one degree shift. There will be times when you are called to make a change and the process will be comforting and obvious. During these times, being with fire will seem as easy as being at a campfire: you will be able to stay and be with the sensations that arise as you make the shift. Yet there will be other times when making a change feels more like walking into a forest fire: you know you need to make the shift, but doing so feels scary, unfamiliar, or uncomfortable. You may interpret the situation as being too intense, too big, too hot, too challenging, and your instinct might be to run away.

Sometimes, life presents situations that are challenging. I refer to staying in these situations or with our feelings when life gets hot as *sitting in the fire*. It is learning to accept feelings of discomfort or struggle, and being with them even when you want to leave, avoid, or deny them. It is the discipline to see an experiment through, whether it is saying yes to your dreams, creating a healthy relationship with appropriate boundaries, resolving a conflict, or delving into the inquiries throughout this book.

Yoga can be a practice of sitting in the fire: getting comfortable being uncomfortable. This can mean staying in an experiment or real-life situation when it gets challenging, or remaining open and curious rather than getting stuck in the idea that life has to be a certain way. It can also mean examining your life with a level of detail you've never tried before. It can simply mean to stay to let the transformation occur.

I know plenty of people who seek out opportunities for sitting in the fire because they love a challenge. If you are this type of person, you may find it is easy to jump right into many of the inquiries. However, it's also totally normal to feel uncomfortable while you're doing the inquiries. You may find that they bring up old stories, old wounds, or old ways of being. At times these experiments can feel a lot like Rolfing, the deep-tissue manual therapy that can be quite intense, almost painful in the moment, yet afterward you notice the benefits of the experience. When the outcome of a one degree shift results in more ease, connection, space, sweetness, or increased awareness, you'll see why the momentary discomfort of the inquiry, the sitting in the fire, will be worth the effort.

Yet many of us do not know how to sit in the fire, and because of this, we can unconsciously sabotage our ability to shift. For instance, I'm always up to try something new, including fire walking. I didn't believe anyone could actually get burned walking across the hot embers. I thought, "Why would so many people do it if they could actually get hurt?" Then I attended a workshop where I was going to get a chance to try it for myself. The facilitators were there to support us as we walked across the coals. Before each of us walked across the coals, one of the facilitators instructed us to say aloud, "Cool moss, cool moss, cool moss." As we walked we were told not to stop until we were on the other side. So when it was my turn, I said yes to the experience and chanted, "Cool moss, cool moss, cool moss," and I went straight across.

The next day I saw a woman with a badge that said, "I'm a fire-walker." The eight-year-old in me piped up and I jokingly asked, "I'm a firewalker, too. Where's my badge?" She responded, "You don't want a badge. You only get one if you burned yourself while you were walking across the coals."

As it turned out, this woman didn't skillfully engage with

the experiment: she walked halfway across the fire when the self-sabotaging part of her mind freaked out and she just stopped moving. That was the exact moment when she burned her feet.

I didn't need to literally walk across burning coals to learn about the power of a one degree shift or to learn about sitting in the fire, and neither will you. However, when you say yes to transformation, you will benefit from learning how to skillfully sit in the fire, make shifts, and set a new course for a new direction.

Become the Diamond

Another way of thinking about sitting in the fire is comparing it to the process of perturbation, a scientific model for determining the amount of pressure that a piece of coal needs to endure in order to turn into a diamond. In some ways, sitting in the fire is that same thing. You're going to experience a certain amount of pressure or discomfort if you want to transform. Are you willing to sit in the fire in order to get to the other side, to really sparkle and find an inner and outer radiance, and reveal the gem you are?

Facing Your Gremlins

It takes courage and resilience to take a deep look at how you respond to life when it feels unfamiliar or gets uncomfortable. You may find that you've been creating a plethora of excuses, obstacles, or whole narratives to avoid sitting in the fire. These can be your gremlins: the ideas and instincts we all have that keep us from making change and that want to preserve the status quo. It is the part of you that holds on to and expresses your fears.

Gremlins are afraid of letting go of old habits even when they clearly don't serve us. They can keep you from stepping into the mystery of transformation because they want to preserve the comfortable, old version rather than seeing what you could possibly blossom into. They act as an inner critic (which I refer to as your critical mind later in the book), and can be judgmental of you and others. Your gremlin can also create beliefs and stories that aren't true, yet convince you that they are.

Every time you think of a worst-case scenario, your gremlins have gotten hold of you. They see the world as a problem rather than an experiment to enjoy. They are the voices in your head that say, "No, no, no, don't do that, you can't do that. You're not good enough, it will never work out, you're too young, you're too old. Don't bother changing." Sometimes your gremlins are the voices that don't even belong to you: they were formed from the perspective, commentary, and opinions of others. Regardless of where they come from, when we listen to our gremlins and take their messages at face value, we can get stuck in the riptide and miss out on an opportunity for transformation.

That said, our gremlins are not our enemies. They most likely developed as a means to protect you. It's quite possible that at some point in your life something may have happened that forced you to create an explanation for circumstances that were painful or that you didn't know how to navigate. So rather than creating more hostility by treating the gremlins as enemies, we can recognize the role they play. If you can do this, then your gremlins will be your allies: they help you see where you could put your attention and make valuable one degree shifts.

ONE DEGREE SHIFT INQUIRY:
Recognizing Your Gremlins

It's almost guaranteed that life will present some challenges where your gremlins will show up. This experiment will help you recognize your gremlins and see their patterns so you know how to respond to them if they appear. This knowledge will help you sit in the fire and allow transformation to take its course.

Draw, collage, or write down your thoughts on how you would express your gremlin. Be specific:

• What does your gremlin look like?
• Does your gremlin have a name?
• What does your gremlin say?
• How does your gremlin affect your life?
• How has it supported you this far?
• What have you learned from your gremlin?
• How can your gremlin be your ally?
• How do you want to treat your gremlin?

What Do You Do When Life Gets Hot?

Our gremlins can come out and play when life gets uncomfortable, feels unfamiliar, when we are called to make a shift, or when we need to put in some extra effort to finish a project or resolve a conflict. Simply, they can keep you from sitting in the fire. While this may make you feel safe in the moment, it doesn't support your efforts to co-create your existence, or actively participate in your own growth.

The following four types of gremlins are common ways we block our own growth opportunities and bypass being uncomfortable. With this better understanding of why you escape when things begin to heat up, you can learn how to sit in the fire—how to stay deeply connected, how to remain resourceful, how to keep believing in yourself, and how to keep reminding yourself that you are choosing this not for self-torture but because you actually believe in something.

Scenario #1: The Avoider

Gremlins can convince you to leave or flee when life gets challenging or hot, to abandon the fire altogether rather than tolerating the uncomfortableness of staying in a situation that is not easy. There are plenty of people who, when faced with a challenge or when things aren't going the way they want, choose to bail and walk away rather than keep going. They may leave when faced with a momentary bump in the road, like when the honeymoon period in a relationship is over, or when the dream job no longer seems so dreamy.

One potential underlying reason why people are avoidant is that sitting in the fire requires facing emotions that they might have never had to deal with. Many of us don't know how to be with our emotions, so instead of staying and exploring them we turn away, shut down, and limit our experiences. We can be so afraid of our feelings or deem ourselves unequipped to tolerate them that we can respond to life like the walking dead, where we avoid feeling altogether. Whether it's fear, sadness, anger, joy, intimacy, or love, just *staying* with any of these emotions can be the act of sitting in the fire.

Yoga teaches that part of what makes life a beautiful journey is that we get the opportunity to feel a spectrum of emotions that creates richness and nuance in our lives, yet so many people limit themselves by reducing how they feel to just good or bad, happy or sad. In a sense our emotions are like a color palette which can stand alone, be combined, and paint the vast complexities and beauty of the human experience. We can equate our emotions to flavors, a juiciness of life that can be mixed, evoked, and fully tasted and savored. While there are many ways to look at our emotional landscape, the *rasas*, meaning juice or sap, derived from Indian dance and theater, focus on nine basic emotions:

- *Sringara:* Passion, love
- *Shanta:* Peace, calm
- *Hasya:* Joy, humor, lightness
- *Adbhuta:* Wonder, curiosity, awe
- *Vira:* Courage
- *Karuna:* Compassion
- *Raudra:* Anger, irritation
- *Bhayanaka:* Fear, doubt, insecurity
- *Vibhasta:* Disgust

Part of sitting in the fire is learning to have a healthy relationship with any of these emotions rather than avoiding them. Often when you are called to change or shift, the first feeling you might experience is detachment or resistance. And when we feel either of these emotions we may think, "I must be going the wrong way," or "This decision can't be right." However, these emotions can actually be an indicator that you are heading in the right direction, because both detachment and resistance can be gremlins that promote avoidance rather than change! Whenever I am called to a one degree shift and experience a feeling of detachment or resistance, I try to get extra curious about these feelings. I'll ask myself, "Is this emotion just a gremlin trying to hijack my growth?"

Joseph Campbell, the famous mythologist, writer, and lecturer, is best known for articulating the notion of the hero's (or heroine's) journey. If you haven't read his book *The Hero with a Thousand Faces*, you might recognize his concepts, which have been incorporated into almost every movie you've ever seen where the hero or heroine goes on a quest: think *Lord of the Rings* or the original *Star Wars*. You know what happens. Campbell writes that anytime we are called to adventure, we will first experience a *refusal of the call*: life is trying to get your attention to change, but your gremlin says that you are not ready or capable, or that you don't need to go. However, when you know that there is a real, desirable outcome on the other side, or that the adventure will be so compelling—you can silence your gremlins or place them aside, and decide to go.

For instance, if you are struggling in a relationship, you might realize that you need to have a difficult conversation. Initially you might feel resistant to being honest about your wants and desires. However, if you are able to recognize that the resistance can be a gremlin that is holding you back, you can acknowledge it, and have the difficult conversation anyway. You might be surprised that you were able to handle riding the waves of the emotions that came up before and during the conversation, and that having the conversation cleared up the problem so that you can move forward in your relationship.

When a seemingly intolerable emotion or the desire to leave a challenging situation presents itself, you don't have to face sitting in the fire alone: you can always ask for help. In chapter 5, you'll learn more about who you can lean on in your community. For now, know that there are plenty of people you already know who can be there for you: to cheer you on, or remind you why you are choosing to sit in the fire. Though no one can walk your path for you, your community can be there as a witness. They can hold you and care for you when your journey seems too much—and cheer you on when you have done the work.

ONE DEGREE SHIFT INQUIRY:
Embracing Your Emotions

- What emotions are challenging to be with?
- What have I been avoiding, and what has the impact been?
- What do I care enough about that I would be willing to sit in the fire to see what lies on the other side?
- Am I willing to sit in the fire simply for the experience, regardless of the final outcome?
- Think of a challenging time in your life when you stayed in the fire and there was a positive outcome. What did that experience teach you?

Scenario #2: The Denier

Gremlins can also convince you that everything about your life is just *fine*: there is no shift that needs to be made, there is nothing that needs to be changed. If you are in a constant state of denial, you won't recognize when transformation needs to happen. This is a particularly tricky gremlin because there are so many ways that people deny dealing with their challenges.

Some people are in denial when they refuse to see or take responsibility for their role in a particular problem. These deniers can shut down or refuse to engage in a conversation; for instance, these are the people who cannot see their role in how we are negatively impacting the health of our planet with the choices we make. Others get defensive about the way their life is going and claim that someone else is the cause of the problem.

Denial can also feel uncomfortable. You might not be able to put your finger on the problem that you are avoiding, and at the same time you might feel an uncomfortableness that you can't quite understand. In response, you might fill that void by working too much, or spending endless hours distracting yourself online, or overexercising, or overeating. Each of these activities might be the way you dissipate the uncomfortable heat.

For instance, I have a friend who recognized that her marriage wasn't the partnership she had envisioned, and asked her husband if he would go to marriage counseling. At first he was willing and open. But as soon as the therapist told him that part of the problem with their marriage was his responsibility, he simply couldn't accept the feedback. Instead, he continued to list all of the reasons why his wife was creating the problems in their marriage.

In this case, her husband's gremlin was keeping him in the dark, and he was not able to own his part of the demise of their marriage. Though she was willing to do the work and sit in the fire for the possibility of repairing their connection, his denial forced her to make the challenging choice to leave.

ONE DEGREE SHIFT INQUIRY:
Point the Finger

- Where are you recognizing that there is a problem and you don't see how you are contributing to it?
- What if you could pause and, for a moment, try on the perspective that you may have a role in the problem?
- What's one small shift you could make to take responsibility and be part of the solution?

Scenario #3: The 95 Percenter

Sometimes we think that we are doing what it takes to sit in the fire, but what we are actually doing is just sitting *next to* the fire—we are experiencing the heat, yet to actually make a shift we need to really put ourselves fully in. This occurs when you are willing to do some of the work to create change, but when the feelings get too intense or the work gets too difficult you stop and/or leave. I call this gremlin the 95 percenter inspired by my teacher and friend Holly McCormack. The problem is that a situation or a feeling usually gets to be the hottest just before a transformation is about to occur.

Staying in the fire to the end can be difficult because it goes against our nature: we are evolutionarily hardwired to avoid pain and discomfort and move toward pleasure and joy. This is why so many of us have the ability to step up for 95 percent of the journey toward change, but start to waver before we get to the end. The last 5 percent often requires enormous effort and can take the most dedication. Imagine how disappointing it would be if every caterpillar left its cocoon right before it was about to spread its new wings as a butterfly.

Yoga teaches the concept of *tapas*, which can mean discipline, dedication, and devotion. There are many ways we can embrace discipline, whether it's committing to a daily movement practice, choosing to follow a healthier lifestyle, creating personal boundaries, or letting go of unhealthy friendships, old habits, or destructive behaviors. These decisions can be both compelling and frightening; either way, to make a shift will most likely take a level of sustained dedication. For example, when I trained for a Half Ironman, there were many days I did not want to train, yet I knew I had to do the work that it took so I could complete the race. Remembering tapas motivated me to say yes to my desire to compete in this race, and then show up and practice every day, riding the waves of comfort and discomfort.

Some of the inquiries in this book might be easy for you, and others may be a bit more challenging. There might be times when you feel like you really did show up 100 percent. Other times, you may not. If the outcome isn't what you desired, regardless of your level of input, you can always try again. And again. That is the beauty of living yoga: we are not expecting perfection; it is simply a path for people who are sincerely interested in showing up to their lives.

Life *is* change, and we always have a beautiful opportunity to remain open. To do so, we can become stronger so that we can be able to withstand a certain level of rigor so we can stay engaged when it gets challenging. When you experience the last 5 percent and tap into your dedication, discipline, and resiliency, even when it gets to be grueling, you can begin to transform. This willingness to stay and transform naturally leads to an increase in awareness about yourself, allows you to better self-reflect, and ultimately to more skillfully ride the waves of life. Whether you are "coming up to the edge" of a job or a relationship, even as your gremlins appear with doubt or disbelief, you can lock into your desire and stay the course. Though we can never truly know how something will turn out, my hope is that as you put yourself into different experiments, you will see a real difference between *before* and *after*.

So much of life is like childbirth, or birthing anything into fruition, whether it's a career, a relationship, a dream. Often, the most intense time of a natural labor is during what is referred to as the *transition*—when your entire body can feel like it is on fire, and you can't imagine that you can take any more heat, but with just one more breath, and one more push, you have a beautiful newborn baby in your arms, and the intense discomfort was worth it. And although during labor women don't have the choice to walk away, too many people walk away from the heat right before their transition.

Sitting in the fire doesn't always require a Herculean effort or have to mean working extra hard; sometimes it can just mean working more skillfully. Often people think when they are caught in a riptide of life or stuck in some rut that by working hard they will get themselves out. That's when you'll hear people say, "Look how hard I am working," yet at the same time they are frustrated because their hard work isn't producing the desirable result or moving them toward the change they are longing for. The more important question to reflect upon can be, "Is what I'm doing working? Is it supporting me to get me out of the riptide?" If the answer is no, then you'll realize that paddling harder or working harder is not enough to create change. Instead, you'll need to shift, try something different, or put yourself in another experiment to make progress or achieve the desired result.

ONE DEGREE SHIFT INQUIRY:
The 100% Effort

- Where in your life can tapas support you making a shift? Where are you only showing up 95 percent?
- What would showing up 100 percent look like? What needs to change?
- Where are you working hard and not seeing results? Where are you not skillfully working? What is one thing you could shift?

Sometimes, You Have to Walk Away

There is no rulebook for how long someone should stay in the fire…it is an experiment. There will be times when you need to stay longer than you want because it can take time for transformation to occur. And if the heat is too hot to handle, and you walk away from the fire too early this time, it is almost guaranteed that life will present other opportunities to try again.

When life gets hot you are also invited to practice the yoga teaching *ahimsa*—we are not to cause unnecessary harm to ourselves or others. Sometimes our emotions can feel super intense. We can remember that they are just emotions, not actual physical pain, and in reality we can tolerate them as we experience them. We can actually stay with them as long as we decide to do so. It's entirely up to you: you have to live your life; no one else gets to decide when you've had too much.

You are always in charge of your life, and you get to decide how much sensation and emotion you can tolerate. There will be times when you're not going to love your job, and you're not always going to be happy with your relationships. The key is to discern the difference between sitting in the fire for the sake of a better outcome, or staying in a harmful situation. Remember why you are sitting in the fire in the first place. The point might be to increase your life force, enhance the greater good, or become more authentic or more free: all valid reasons for sitting in the fire even when you are uncomfortable. Staying in an abusive relationship, or staying in a job that depletes your life force, will not make you a better person, and once you recognize the situation, you are free to make the choice to leave.

Get yourself out of any situation where you are being harmed or if you are in emotional distress that seems unsafe. There is a difference between pain and intense sensation—when you experience pain you stop, and if you feel a new sensation, even if it is intense, you keep going. No one can decide for you how hot is too hot; you have to take care of yourself.

A question to ask yourself when you are questioning if you are experiencing pain or a sensation is, "Am I creating a crime against wisdom by sitting in the fire?" If you are, be courageous enough to stop, and be willing to reassess the situation and try a different experiment. Err on the side of caution.

Scenario #4: The Victim

Sometimes, gremlins appear when you say yes to sitting in the fire, but you see yourself as the victim to the circumstance. When it gets hot the victim often forgets that they knowingly put themselves in the experiment. Victims often sees themselves as suffering, and create excuses for why they are disempowered and don't have a choice. The gremlin comes across as a complaint, like, "This is so annoying; it's so hot I can't stay here." The victim might also say something like, "Why is everything always so hard for me?" or "I can't believe I have to do this." They forget that it was their decision to walk this path of transformation.

So often what keeps people from transforming is that they become a victim to a story from their past and are unwilling to let it go. The stories of abandonment, of not being lovable or worthy, can fuel your gremlins, which provide the false evidence that you do not have a choice or the power to change. This is when the voice of the gremlin can say things like, "If they only knew my story, then they would know why I can't do this." These gremlins may convince you that you aren't strong enough, or that you can't do what it takes to transform. They may tell you all the reasons why it is harder for you to change than for someone else. We buy into these gremlins rather than focusing on our potential and what is possible on the other side of the fire.

ONE DEGREE SHIFT INQUIRY:
Identifying the Victim

- Is there a situation where you are blaming someone or some circumstance for your misfortune?
- Do you feel like there is nothing you can do to shift your circumstance?
- Do you feel like the world is out to get you?
- Do you feel powerless in different types of situations or relationships?
- Do you see your behaviors in others that you feel are victimized?
- Is there a place where you may be making yourself a victim to a situation? Is it possible to own that possibility for the sake of transformation?
- What can you shift to feel empowered?
- Instead of blaming others or the situation, what could you focus on instead?

The Seven Steps to Sitting in the Fire

When a situation arises and you know you have to sit in the fire, there are skillful ways to do so. Yoga teaches us that we can practice sitting in the fire on the mat by having a *sadhana*, or practice. We can create a different type of sadhana for sitting in the fire when life gets hot off the mat. Here are seven steps that can support you to more willingly sit in the fire:

Step One: Notice

Usually there is a feeling of refusal to the call, or a desire to pull away from the situation, followed by a willingness to seek out what is on the other side, and to stay.

Step Two: Connect

Begin by connecting to your breath. Take a deep breath and allow yourself to experience the moment. Bring awareness to your feet on the earth and the ground. When you feel present, connect to the reason you are choosing to sit in the fire: What is the outcome that you are committed to more than alleviating this experience of momentary discomfort?

Step Three: Observe

Simply observe your thoughts, feelings, and any internal commentary with compassion. The ability to observe a situation without taking an action can be a shift in itself. The practice is to just notice the sensations you feel without responding. In this moment of observation, you are able to recognize your gremlins and the stories they create that may not be true.

Step Four: Shift Perspectives

Ask yourself, "Am I committing a crime against wisdom by sitting in the fire?" If the answer is yes, stop and remember *ahimsa*: do no harm. If the answer is no, and your gremlins are lurking, the antidote is to create a new perspective and reframe the experience you are having sitting in the fire. You can try on a different perspective and see how it creates a new reality or another way of being while you sit in the fire.

Then, ask yourself, "What is my perspective about this current situation? Am I willing to shift my perspective to make sitting in the fire more inviting?" For instance, if you believe that you are a victim, you could try on a new perspective such as, "I am strong and I can be with the sensations." If you are experiencing the perspective that sitting in the fire is miserable, try on, "Sitting in the fire provides me an opportunity to prove I can be with a challenge." Or, instead of "I can't do this," try a simple, yet profound shift of, "Yes, I can."

Think of your new perspective as a mantra, a word tool you can use whenever your gremlins are affecting your decision-making.

Step Five: Create a Boundary with Your Gremlin

This new perspective can be solidified when you establish a clear boundary with your gremlins. The truth is, you are the one in charge, not the critical self-sabotaging gremlin. Imagine you are drawing a line that the gremlin cannot cross, and when that gremlin tries to creep in again, you simply notice, repeat your mantra, and say yes to your new perspective as many times as you need to until you have accomplished what you have set out to shift.

Step Six: Allow the Experience to Occur

With your new perspective, you can be with the fire in a new way. You start to understand what it means to get comfortable being uncomfortable, and you may find that you are more equipped to sit in the fire than you ever thought. You have the inner resilience to see the experience through to the end. You walked across the coals successfully and unscathed.

Step Seven: Embody What You Have Transformed Into

This practice allows you to collect new information and data about yourself. You are not the same person you were before. Live as this new version of yourself and have confidence that when life presents uncomfortable opportunities to shift, you can meet the challenge gracefully.

Whenever a challenge arises, put yourself in the experiment using the Seven Steps. Journal about your experience. What did you learn about yourself? Your gremlin? What worked? What didn't?

Let's say you need to have an honest conversation with a friend that you imagine will be difficult. First, notice if you feel a resistance to having the talk. Then, take a deep breath and find a way to connect to the reason you want to have the conversation. Observe if your gremlins come up, including thoughts like, "I can't do this," or "This is too hard," or any of the other worst-case scenarios that come rushing into your head. Be compassionate with your gremlin that is trying to hijack the moment. Once you have observed them, you then can shift into a new perspective of how you want to be while having the conversation: how you can better handle the discomfort that may arise. To live into this new perspective, say your mantra to yourself as you create a boundary with your gremlin. With your gremlins put aside, you can now have the conversation with a new sense of confidence.

This practice is not a one-time event—you might need to do this multiple times even within a single conversation, depending on how loud your gremlins are. Each time you sit in the fire, you can create a new story that overwrites what the gremlin had been saying. You are able to collect new data about yourself or the situation, and you'll find that you are better able to recognize your gremlins.

The ability to sit in the fire can have a lasting impact that goes well beyond the momentary event. When you learn to sit in the fire and transform your gremlins into new, helpful beliefs, riding the waves gets that much easier.

We Are in It Together

When you have sat in the fire, your level of empathy for others increases because you can relate to what it took to go through a transformation—the resiliency, discipline, or dedication to stay when it was uncomfortable. You gain a deeper respect for those who chose to stay for the sake of the transformation or for those who are learning to sit in the fire for the first time. You have a greater ability to relate, to connect, and to offer support to these individuals who are choosing to stay in the heat because they are committed to growth. By reflecting on your own journey, you can both be there and honor the process for others.

Create a New Belief: You Are Not Your Gremlins

When you sit in the fire and are able to create a boundary with your gremlins, or compost their energy into fuel, it can naturally lead to creating a new belief about yourself and your abilities: you may feel that you are now stronger than your gremlins. You will begin to recognize when they show up, and then can say to yourself, "Oh, that was just a gremlin." Or, "That was just a thought. I am more than that thought; I am not that thought. I'm not that gremlin and I don't have to beat up the gremlins; I don't have to think they're bad and wrong. I am able to recognize the gremlin is just a gremlin. It's not actually who I am."

When you realize all that you are not, you are able to start to step into who you are. The revelation may be that "I am strong," "I am resilient," or "I am capable" when the gremlins are no longer in charge and dictating your inner dialogue.

ONE DEGREE SHIFT INQUIRY:
Creating Boundaries

Practicing creating a boundary with your gremlins is one of the best gifts you can give yourself! This radical act can change the course of your life—forever. You might first ask yourself:

- Where in your life do you know that you would benefit from creating some kind of boundary? A few examples might be:
  1. Eliminating a habit you know isn't serving you for seven days—try steering clear of gossiping, sugar, television, or social media.
  2. Creating a boundary with negative people.
  3. Creating a boundary with saying yes all the time, when you actually mean no.

- What do you imagine would shift in a positive way if you created that boundary?
- If you were to do this experiment again what advice would you give yourself?

The Gremlin Action Plan

It is almost guaranteed that anytime you are called to make a change or sit in the fire, the gremlins will come rushing in and ask, "Are you sure about that?" A Gremlin Action Plan (GAP) can help you meet your gremlins head-on, for the sake of staying—when it gets hard, when it is uncomfortable, or when you are unsure what the next step is—in the experiment long enough to transform.

This practice can illuminate your coping mechanisms and help you build relationships with the various tactics you already use to hold yourself back from creating change. The plan is meant to set up parameters for how you want to respond when your gremlins show up when a situation gets hot or challenging and you care so much that you want to stay.

A Gremlin Action Plan is a simple awareness practice. It prepares you for potential gremlins that might arise during an experiment, and provides steps you can take in case they do.

1. What is the experiment you want to put yourself in? For example, you might decide you want to start meditating every day.

2. What is the potential gremlin that could show up? What might they say? For instance, when your alarm goes off, you rationalize why staying in bed is better/more important than meditating. That rationalization is your gremlins saying, "Oh, let's start tomorrow; isn't the bed so comfy and warm?"

3. What could you say to your gremlins instead of listening to them? Start by thinking what is so compelling about the experiment you want to put yourself in that you are willing to face your gremlins. Then, state your response, i.e.: "Thank you, gremlins, for showing up, but I am going to get up now and meditate so that I can practice starting my day more consciously and experience more peace, kindness, and freedom throughout the day."

4. What else could you do to face your gremlins? What

support do you need or what actions could you take that will send your gremlins running? For instance, I could ask my three closest friends if they want to participate in a morning meditation practice. Or I could ask them to be my accountability buddies—and I could text them each day and let them know I meditated. Or I could set ten alarms to go off on my phone and keep the phone on the other side of the room. The key is to get specific and have a plan for the moments when your gremlins want to take over.

Transforming Your Gremlin Energy into Fuel

One of the aims of yoga is to transform fears, wounds, hurts, and stories into fuel; the transformative power of shifting "gremlin energy" into the potent life force necessary to live more vibrantly in the world. One positive outcome of recognizing your gremlins and learning to be with them—and not be overtaken by them—is that you can detach yourself from their grip, transforming their protectionism into something more useful. Sitting in the fire creates this same fuel, which can make the experience easier every time you try.

The ancient yoga practitioners used to create rituals and ceremonies with the intention of bringing up their gremlins (though they didn't refer to them as gremlins; sometimes they are referenced as an "inner animal" or "inner demon"). One practice was visiting a cemetery on a new moon. The night would be pitch black and the yogi would stay awake all night in the dark, alone, to intentionally stir up any fears, doubts, and insecurities. When the morning came, after facing their gremlins throughout the night, many would feel invincible: composting their fears into fuel led to a feeling of vitality, confidence, and empowerment which carried into other aspects of their life.

ONE DEGREE SHIFT INQUIRY:
Sat Nam

Rather than going to a cemetery, you can create your own gremlin energy transformation ritual right on the yoga mat. In the yoga tradition there are practices called *kriyas*, cleansing rituals or cleansing practices. A kriya can churn your inner world so that you face your gremlins and turn them into fuel.

This practice, *Sat Nam*, is a kriya that allows you to face your gremlins if they come up and use them as renewing fuel. The world *sat* can mean truth, and *nam* can mean identity. Sat Nam is therefore an invitation to step into your truth—who you are beyond your gremlins. The practice allows you to notice your gremlins and the ways in which you can ride the waves of sensations and thoughts. During the exercise you are invited to create a new story by breaking the barriers and limitations you place on yourself, and collecting new data.

Sat Nam can be physically strenuous, and might produce a burning sensation. If you question whether you should try this practice, ask your doctor, create a variation for yourself, or simply don't do it. For instance, I typically lead this exercise for twenty-two minutes; for some three minutes would be a great place to start. Remember *ahimsa*: do no harm!

• Stand up tall with your feet hip distance apart.
• You will be repeating the words *Sat Nam* as a mantra.

If it does not feel comfortable or appropriate for you, create your own mantra. It could be something like, "I am powerful" or "I bow to my truth."

- Decide on an amount of time that feels like a challenge, and set a timer. Make an agreement with yourself that if at any point you feel like you are hurting yourself you will immediately stop. There is a difference between pain and intense sensation—pain you stop, sensation, you keep going. If you can't decipher which is which in the moment, err on the side of caution—stop if you think you are harming yourself.

- Briskly bring your arms out to the sides and raise your hands up and over your head, forming a circle with your arms where one hand is on top of the other. Then with the same force lower your arms and bring your elbows down by your side. When you bring the arms up say "Sat," and when you bring your elbows down by your side say "Nam." Repeat this movement and mantra continuously for the allotted time you chose.

- When the timer rings, keep your arms lifted—this is an amazing opportunity to feel! Take the next two minutes to slowly lower your arms. Without making sound, close your eyes, or soften your gaze and take the next few minutes to witness your feelings. You might feel emotions moving through you, you may feel powerful, you might even notice a gremlin trying to come in and say that you didn't do it *good enough*. If you feel like your gremlins were active during the exercise, don't worry! Part of the experience is to notice when they show up, to hold space for them, and to learn how to work with them in a new way each time they arise. This is why yoga is a practice. It is not about being perfect. Rather, it's about being willing to be in the experiment. You get to try again and again and apply what you learn each time around.

Freedom Is an Inside Job

One concept of yoga is *svatantrya*—a quality of consciousness which can be translated as independence, freedom of will, or one's own choice. Yoga teaches that freedom is our birthright. To me, this means that freedom can live and thrive within boundaries. Too often we struggle because we don't think we have power, so we feel imprisoned by a circumstance, another person, or a belief. Yet if we see that our power is the ability to shift our perspective of the boundaries, we can change our internal experience and access our internal freedom. While you can't always control the external world, you can take responsibility for how you respond to your inner world, and whatever is happening in the external world. These are the keys to freedom.

You do not need to study ancient texts, sit for hours of meditation, twist your body in intricate yoga postures, or do anything else to be free—it is your inherent birthright because freedom can be sourced from within. Sitting in the fire is one way to recognize that boundaries are not the cause of a problem, and that they can contain infinite possibilities. The boundary of a canvas only shows us how much space you have to paint; it doesn't dictate what can be painted. The boundary of a monogamous relationship doesn't have to be seen as a limitation; it has the possibility to create greater intimacy and depth.

Sadly, what happens too often is that people do not use their keys to get out of their "imprisonment," and instead lock themselves in and throw the keys out. Yet when we shift our belief to recognize that we were never in prison, that the door was never locked, and that some of our anguish created false stories that we interpreted as truth, that's when we realize that freedom is an inside job. When we recognize this new truth, we can start to transform our gremlins, create new beliefs, and take ownership of the shifts we want to make.

ONE DEGREE SHIFT INQUIRY:
What Keeps You Imprisoned?

Many people are willing to work overtime to convince themselves and others why they aren't free. You can use the concept of *svatantrya* as a way to check in when you are feeling out of alignment:

- Where are you convincing yourself or others that you aren't free? You could look at your health, your finances, your relationships, your family, your work, or your obligations.
- Where do you give your power away to other people or circumstances? What is the impact? Do you let other people make decisions for you? Do you silence yourself instead of speaking up?
- Which of your gremlins are creating a false sense of self-imprisonment?
- What shifts when you see that even in circumstances that you don't like or agree with, you still have power?

Jump into Your One Degree Revolution

I used to skydive . . . a lot. One of my favorite parts of skydiving was to take people out for the first time. I love watching others go through the whole process, beginning with the nervous anticipation of the jump, then as we go through the instructional class to the plane ride up, and up and up! As the plane climbs higher and higher, most people's gremlins start to arise—whether it be fear, or nervous laughter; or they go into absolute silence and terror starts to take over. Sometimes, they begin to create the worst-case scenario in their head—that their chute won't open and they will die. When the door opens and it is just about their time to jump, they have a choice to either let their gremlins take over and dominate the experience, or acknowledge them, ignore them, or invite them to jump with them. These are three ways you can be with any of your gremlins; acknowledge that they are there, totally ignore them, or recognize and befriend them. The power lives within you to choose.

To me, skydiving is the perfect metaphor for transformation. You choose to say yes to the call of adventure, your life, or whatever it is that you are stepping into. When a feeling of detachment or resistance or any other gremlin arises—you can be with them and continue to face these gremlins as you stand on the edge of the plane. When you finally jump, you are jumping into the unknown—the joy and the terror. While you are in the air, you can see the world from an entirely different perspective. And when you finally land, you are forever changed. You have faced your gremlins, and have reclaimed their energy and composted it into fuel. The feeling of "I can do anything" takes over and every cell in your body is vibrating. You feel totally alive. And feelings of hope, possibility, anticipation, and excitement are tattooed in your memory.

I once took Erica, one of my best friends, skydiving for her first time. We were in a very small plane; there were only five of us, includ-ing the pilot. Erica was attaching herself to a skydive master who was going to dive with her. Once you're connected to the master, there's not much for you to do: basically you get to the edge of the plane and the master will count to three, and on three, you jump out of the plane.

It was clear that Erica's gremlins were activated. She even mouthed to me the words "I don't want to go." She was standing on the edge of the doorway, and before the skydive master was able to count to three, she tried to turn around and jump back into the plane. But the skydive master took her and just jumped out of the plane with her. I thought to myself, "What have I done to my best friend!" For-tunately, when she got to the bottom, she was thrilled to have done it.

There are times in life where you throw yourself willingly out of the plane, and then there are other times when life seems to just throw you out. As you walk a path of yoga and journey through this book, I hope you are a willing participant.

This is your life, and only you can decide what is right for you. And, if you are willing to say yes to your potential and ability to savor the pre-cious gift of life, and face your fears, face your gremlins, you then realize that you a taking a stand for your life and your own transformation.

Are you interested in your own potential, and do you believe that you can transform, even if you don't know how to do it? Are you ready to be a willing participant to your own growth and evolution? If so, let's get ready to jump.

Courageous one,
jump into your own transformation,
heart wide open.
One, two, three . . .

3

Dare to Be Your Authentic Self

You matter.
Your life matters.
You belong.

Yoga teaches that being authentic can lead to a happier, more intimate relationship with life. I know that this is easier said than
done; authenticity can be a big ask. The truth is if you asked anyone if they feel like they're 100 percent authentically themselves,
100 percent of the time, most would say "hardly ever." We juggle
many roles every day, and each comes with a prescribed set of rules.
We're supposed to be serious working professionals, authoritative
yet kind parents, loving partners, or diligent students. Yet sometimes
we want to be playful children, introspective thinkers, or driven ac-
tivists. Too often, we overidentify with these roles, and forget or
push aside who we really are at our core.

Part of the quest for authenticity is figuring out how we align what we say, think, feel, and do—and also discover work that gives us meaning, relationships that are fulfilling, and unveiling our life purpose and our values. Yet so often what we say or do is actually vastly different from what we are thinking or feeling. This lack of alignment can create anxiety, exhaustion, or depression.

For instance, many people struggle because they live in a state of illusion or delusion—they view their life through a lens of fear, fantasy, and distortion. Many fears, such as a fear of speaking up, a fear of heights or flying occur when people view a situation thinking the worst-case scenario will happen—they crash the plane in their mind before it has even taken off. It's like being put in a room that has a coil of rope in the corner, yet you have decided that it's a venomous snake. When you are looking through a similarly distorted lens at your life or what's going on around you, as in a fun house, and create judgments about yourself or others, you aren't giving your authentic self a fighting chance to shine.

You might be living inside a distortion if you are knowingly not telling the truth about some part of your life—to yourself or to others. The fear of hurting others, or living with the ramifications of who you want to be, can hold you back from being authentic. You might realize that your sexual preference, or identity, is different than what your friends and family think. You might realize that you're in a totally unfulfilling career, or a draining and destructive relationship. Yet owning these feelings and coming out to the world as your authentic self could be your one degree shift and could change the course of your life.

Even more important, authenticity means tapping into, and embracing, who you really are. Every moment, of every breath, of every second, of every day, you have the opportunity to appreciate that you are uniquely you. Yet we often fail to recognize the precious gift that we are because we fall into the seduction of comparison. Some people claim they aren't able to fully express their authentic selves because they are afraid of being judged. We rely so heavily on the opinions of others because our culture can be focused on image, social media stimulation, and surface judgments (both positive and negative). It's no wonder that self-image and worth can be heavily influenced by what we think others think about us, instead of relying on the internal potency of who we know we are.

When you compare yourself to others you can fail to recognize your unique gifts, and you can end up feeling worse about yourself. All of a sudden, everyone else is more beautiful or more talented or has a better family life or . . . fill in the blank. I once saw a woman I didn't know hugging my partner and the first thing I noticed was that she was strikingly beautiful. As soon as I saw her, my initial reaction was surprisingly triggering. In that moment an old wound of not feeling beautiful enough was activated, and I was seduced by comparison. When I paused, and checked in with my reaction, I stopped comparing myself to her and I realized that while she brings something beautiful to this lifetime, I also bring my own beauty and gifts forward. My perception of the situation shifted when I started to awaken a sense of gratitude for who I am.

Yoga teaches that when we experience discomfort, and are willing to unpack the lessons underneath it, we're able to heal parts of our wounds and have a greater sense of feeling at home with ourselves and the world around us. Stopping the cycle of vicious comparison is one of the most courageous things you can do. Instead of falling into the seduction of comparison, start to relish who you are and what you bring to the world that is unique. We are not all supposed to have the same type of beauty, or bodies, or intelligence, or humor. Think of it this way: zebras are cool. Zebras are amazing. Now, imagine going on a safari and all you see are zebras. Where are the lions? Where are the giraffes? Where are the jaguars? We need all of the creatures to show up in order to create the beautiful multiplicity of life. The truth is, the world needs you as you really are more than it needs you to be what you are not.

It can feel risky to be authentic around others. At some point most everyone can feel this way. Though we have the ability to be loving and kind, we can also be critical and judgmental. And many of us fear being judged and criticized—so we often don't expose our true selves. If this is the case for most everyone, then we are all walking around hiding our true selves. By diving into the inquiry of authenticity, you might start to see that we're all colluding within a bizarre game of "I'm going to pretend not to be me and you pretend not to be you, and we'll judge and criticize each other anyway."

Instead of judging others, take that energy and create a boundary with that gremlin. Risk being judged (and appreciated!) for who you really are rather than who you are not, and learn to take off your mask and embrace what it means to be your authentic self.

ONE DEGREE SHIFT INQUIRY:
Meeting Authenticity

To begin this quest of authenticity, ask yourself:

- Where is what you say, think, feel, and do out of alignment with how you perceive your most authentic self?

- Are you afraid of fully expressing yourself?
- Are you compromising your values just to fit in?
- Are you showing up differently at home, at work, or with your friends in a way that feels insincere or inauthentic?
- What is the impact?
- What is one thing you could do today to begin to align what you say, think, feel, and do?

Welcome Yourself, Exactly as You Are

It breaks my heart that it takes so many people a lifetime to learn to be welcoming to who they are—that they are lovable, worthy, and whole just as they are. At the same time, I am grateful when it is revealed to them. If you're called to the inquiry of authenticity, be willing to put down your weapons of defensiveness and resistance. Take off the proverbial armor of resistance that's trying to protect you for the sake of getting curious about who you are and who you are evolving into.

Next, you are invited to welcome all of yourself—the parts that you like, and the parts you are learning to like. Welcoming means treating yourself the same way you would treat a guest in your home—you might not like every aspect of this guest, but you would still be kind to them, and show empathy and compassion.

ONE DEGREE SHIFT INQUIRY:
I Welcome Meditation

Begin the day by taking five minutes to try out this simple welcoming meditation that was inspired by my teacher, friend, and colleague Dr. Lorin Roche. You will be welcoming yourself completely, exactly as you are, with the recognition that you are growing, evolving, and learning. You could do this anywhere—while lying in bed, on your yoga mat, or in the shower!

- Begin first by taking three deep breaths.
- Relax your body as much as you can.
- Welcome in the senses for a few moments by listening to sounds around you, the sights you see, what you feel. Welcome everything and expect nothing.
- Say out loud or to yourself, "I welcome all of myself."
- You might find that moving your body in some way allows you to greet yourself more fully. You might reach your arms up to the sky, and then slowly lower your hands in front of your body as you say, "I welcome all of myself." Say this three more times.
- For the next few minutes you will be going on a journey of welcoming different aspects of yourself. Here are a few examples that you can choose from. Be gentle and kind to yourself, and be open to what shows up in your mind!

  ○ I welcome my body.
  ○ I welcome my kindness.

- ○ I welcome my humor.
- ○ I welcome my sadness.
- ○ I welcome my empowered self.
- ○ I welcome my frustration (remember, you are just being welcoming, it does not mean you need to act from this place).
- ○ I welcome the part of me that doesn't want to be welcoming.
- ○ I welcome my fears.
- ○ I welcome my desires.
- ○ I welcome my sexuality.
- ○ I welcome… (continue to fill in different aspects of yourself)

Finish by saying again three times, "I welcome all of myself." Take a few minutes to savor the feeling. Here are a few questions to ask yourself as you transition from this "I Welcome Meditation" to the rest of your day:

- What does it look like to put down your weapons and take off your armor?
- Where can you be more gentle and welcoming with yourself today?
- How can you be more welcoming to others today?

Your Victories

One way you can be gentler toward yourself is choosing to see the many accomplishments you've already had. Go through each year of your life (yes, all of them) and create a journal entry or collage representing your victories and successes. You might find yourself completing this exercise quickly, or it might take you some time: either way, enjoy the process. When you arrive at the present, include each month for the last year. Look how much you've accomplished!

Who You Are vs. Who You Really Are

Part of the journey of living yoga is to know the different parts of yourself: to discover who you are and who you really are. It always makes me laugh when people say to me, "I know you." My response to that is, "Really? I'm just getting to know myself right now."

You can think of *who you are* as how you choose to show up in the world based on your response to outer circumstances. It is the role you play or each part of your personality you want the world to think you have. Fun fact: personality comes from the Latin word "persona," meaning "mask." Often the word was used when there weren't enough actors to fill all the parts in a play; midway through, somebody would put on a persona, or mask, and play a different role.

There can be a big difference between authenticity and personality, and people tend to confuse the two. A personality is the part of ourselves that we show others in our attempt to navigate the world. It explains what we've learned about ourselves over time that works for us. While there is nothing wrong with having a distinct personality, in a sense it's like an outfit. Some days you might want to get dressed up and wear heels; other days, a T-shirt and shorts seem like a great fit. Wearing a mask, or trying on different outfits, is a natural and normal part of being human. Yet you are more than any one mask. You are more than the various aspects of your personality. You are more than the ways in which you have constructed yourself to survive, to feel welcomed or accepted. You are more than the aspects of your personality that don't work anymore, even though you may have developed them in order to cope with challenging life events.

Who you really are is your authentic self, not merely your personality. It is your natural essence, the part of you that isn't attached to a back story. Some traditions of yoga would say that accessing who you really are is a path to your most intimate self, a gateway to having a relationship with the less tangible, more indefinable aspects of life. It is the core of your being which knows you belong in the scheme of a much larger framework.

Yoga teaches that when we strip away our personality, we can discover our authentic nature, who we really are. It is uncovering how we present to the world, as my friend and California-based yoga educator, Katie Brauer, asks, "Who are you when no one's watching?" We inadvertently take on aspects of a personality that were useful at the time yet get in the way of who we can actually become. For example, if a child grew up in a household where she didn't feel loved, she might develop a tough edginess to her personality. This tough exterior may have worked as a way to navigate life, but underneath that may have been a delicate flower desiring love, as her true essence.

Part of the beauty of living yoga is to discover all the layers of who you are. Just because you may have been wounded and created coping mechanisms to survive doesn't mean you have to hold on to them. You may realize, "I don't always need to be the strong one. I don't always need to be the one in charge. I don't always need to be the funny one." What's more, you can take on new aspects of a personality that might serve you better. You may realize, "I'm also the one who sometimes needs help. I'm also the one who sometimes just wants to rest and relax. I'm also the one who can just listen." And at some point these coping mechanisms may no longer serve us, and we can learn how to respond to life rather than react to it. From that place of clearer seeing it is easier to step into the little shifts that will allow us to act in alignment with who we really are.

When everyone around you can see the full range of your humanness, it gives them permission to do the same. That is how we can become a source of inspiration to others, and is reason enough to discover your authentic self! And better still, it leads directly to having more intimate, authentic relationships.

Give Yourself Permission to Be Yourself

One of the beautiful things about being our authentic selves, which includes our personality and our true nature, is that we get to have preferences. I have a preference for conversations that quickly dive beneath the surface; I enjoy knowing what's "really going on" for someone. I have a preference for eating a primarily whole-food, plant-based diet, because I feel more alive when I eat this way. I have a preference for quiet mornings. And at the same time, I realize I am not my preferences. I remind myself that while it is fine to have preferences, I am also a constantly changing and evolving person, and I'm open to being curious about who I am becoming, and how these preferences might change over time.

It is so easy to get overly identified with our preferences, whether it's how we relate to others and the world around us, food choices, who we are attracted to, where we live, or what our favorite season is, etc. When we get stuck in a box we construct rigid walls and forget that there is a world full of wonder out there and so many new flavors of life to try. We forget that we can expand into the more. Our preferences end up being a delicate dance between honoring our individual inclinations and putting ourselves into the inquiry of what else is possible.

ONE DEGREE SHIFT INQUIRY:
Find Your Preferences

We are a part of a huge world and there are lots of ways to live in it. If you stay within the confines of your typical choices, life can become limited and closed. You are invited to "collect data" as an experiment—to learn about what you like and what you don't. So look at your own life and answer the following:

- What are some of your preferences that make you uniquely you? For example, look at how you like the rhythm of your day to go, the way you engage in relationships, or even the climate you like best.
- Where are your preferences actually creating rigid walls that limit your ability to experience new things or connect with different people?
- What is a small shift experiment you could put yourself in to break out of the box of your preferences and try something new?

We are Both Perfect and Evolving

When I was in my late teens, I wasn't comfortable with drastic change. But I remember the moment when I decided I was not going to let this fear rule my life. In college I quit Division 1 swimming—which had been a huge part of my life since I was seven years old (thanks, Russell Mill swim team, where it all began!)—to take an internship in Florida, far from my home, my friends, and my comfort. After that experience, I kept chipping away at this fear. During my twenties and early thirties I moved over twenty times, and in every new location I would take up a new hobby. Whether it was surfing in Florida; living in the woods for three months in Baja Mexico during a National Outdoor Leadership School course; going on a solo trip almost around the world; getting my skydiving license in North Carolina; trying improv in New York City, flower essences in Hawaii, skateboarding in California, or DJ'ing in Boston, I was determined to learn about myself and life. And I did. I studied as many different fields as I could—business, environmental science, transformative leadership, coaching, floral design, Ayurveda, yoga, art/music/dance therapy, conscious communication, whole-food plant-based eating, and positive psychology.

One year I decided to take up pottery. The first project was making little pinch pots that could hold herbs, seeds, and flower petals. I loved to give them as gifts to friends and family. Let's say that the first results were less than stellar. In fact, they weren't good at all. Some of the pinch pots weren't evenly glazed and had tiny cracks. They certainly weren't perfect, but I decided to offer them as gifts anyway. I heard a small voice of doubt that focused on the imperfections I saw in the pots, yet everyone genuinely appreciated them and didn't even notice the flaws I saw. I realized that I had been focusing too much on what I could do better and never paused to recognize the perfection that was right there.

We all might act this way, focusing on what's wrong rather than seeing what's right, right in front of our eyes. Whether it's our education system, or technology, or the yoga world, you name it—most of us could make a list of things that are wrong, broken, or could be improved. Though our criticisms may be accurate, what if part of the solution to fixing these problems was first to see the perfection right in front of us? For instance, while we haven't yet found cures for all chronic diseases, so many people are living longer by incorporating beneficial lifestyle choices and appropriate medical interventions. That doesn't mean we're stopping to look for cures, or searching for the root causes of these diseases.

There is a healthy difference between perfection and good. When I talk about perfection, I don't mean to give the word any moral or ethical weight—I simply mean that whatever exists, exists, and is already perfect in itself. When we look at life through a binary lens where something can either be "good" or "bad," we can be quick to see all that is bad. The pinch pot with the cracks might not be *good*, but it's perfect. If we can pause long enough where we are now, before we criticize, before we focus on what isn't working, is broken or out of alignment, and recognize the perfect piece of art called life that's right in front of us, then we're likely to enjoy life a little more. In fact, we can be the perfect pinch pot, with the cracks and all, and know that we can still evolve into something more, a different perfection.

The yogic concept of *purnatva* is a quality of consciousness that teaches that we are perfect exactly as we are, and at the same time we are evolving into a different form of perfection. For instance, think of yourself as the pinch pot. At what point do you trust that you are enough? That you are perfect just as you are? That you belong, that you matter. Treat yourself and your contributions as a gift, and embrace your perfection while still honoring your potential for learning and growth. Yoga teaches that we are always living on the brink of potential. Like an artist starting off with a slab of wood, clay, or stone, there is endless potential and infinite possibilities of how the raw form will transform into a unique piece of art.

Your authentic self is both perfect as it is and is always evolving into a different perfection. If you believe in potential, it means you can direct your life with greater clarity and a willingness to be in the experiment. The big question is, What do you want to do with this potential?

Yet, too often it seems that people place imaginary or unnecessary limits on themselves. Many of my students have come to me saying, "Well, this is just who I am and I'm always going to be like this." When I hear this, my response is usually the same. I tell them, "Well, up until this point, that might have been true." And then I share the story of the sunflower seed.

A sunflower seed holds all the potential to become a glorious sunflower if it gets water, sunlight, nutrient-dense soil, and is well tended. Both the seed and the flower are equally perfect; they're just different expressions of the same perfection. So whatever you're experiencing in life, trust that there's always more to come. There's always more of life to be revealed because life, like the sunflower, is a continuum.

When you realize that your nature, your essence, your personality is evolving, you can start to have a bigger perspective that maybe there's more going on than what you may see in this moment. When you are open to your potential—what will come in the future—you may recognize that you are connected to the miracle of life that continues all around you: the ocean, flowers, birds, the mountains, sunrises, lakes, rivers, fauna, clouds, and the sky. In every moment, the world is changing and offering herself to all of us to enjoy. And the best place to begin to savor this feast for the senses, to first welcome the evolving perfection, is with you.

For instance, my mother has told me countless times that when I was born she saw me through the lens of perfection. She didn't look at me and say to herself, "Well, if only she had different eyes—then she would be perfect." Too often we look at ourselves and think, "Well, if only . . . I need to fix this flaw."

Wouldn't it be great if we all could look at ourselves through the eyes of *purnatva*, kindness, and love? What becomes available when we can simply experience what we are experiencing, and at the same time enjoy being part of this process, understanding that consciousness wants to evolve into its next perfection?

ONE DEGREE SHIFT INQUIRY:
You Are Perfect and Evolving

Look at yourself through that lens of *purnatva*; i.e. you are perfect, whole, and complete as you are, and evolving into a different perfection.

For the next seven days, begin each morning by looking at yourself in the mirror and allowing yourself to create a boundary with your gremlin, with the part of the mind that can say things less than loving—or the part of the mind that focuses on what you need to "fix." Then, look through the eyes of love and begin to truly see yourself. Allow yourself to soften, breathe, and release unnecessary judgments, and instead look for the ways in which you are like the perfect pinch pot, whole and complete just as you are today. Allow yourself to stay there, in front of the mirror, until you have a moment of recognition.

You can use the concept of *purnatva* as a way to check in when you are feeling out of alignment. Take a moment now and answer the following one degree shift questions:

- What does it mean for you to see yourself as whole, complete, and perfect?
- What would have to shift for you to own that you are already whole, complete, and perfect now?
- What is possible for you now if you fully stood in this truth?
- And at the same time, where can you evolve into a different perfection?

The Five Layers of Being

Looking at the ways you can align what you say, think, feel, and do is a great place to find one degree inquiries for stepping into your authentic self. The yogic tradition offers a valuable map of inquiry to support this process. It proposes the idea that human beings are comprised of five *koshas*, or layers—the physical body, breath body, mental body, witness body (the compassionate observer), and bliss body (the recognition of the interconnectedness of everything)—and that if you take time to explore them, the koshas support the relationship between *who you are* and *who you really are*.

These layers can be looked at independently, but in reality they are interwoven and influence one another. Yet there isn't any one moment when the koshas are fully aligned and working seamlessly forever and ever. Instead, we thrive when we are open to how each of these layers can work more skillfully together; we call this living with integrity.

When this happens, we can experience a sense of flowing with life and feel robust physically, mentally, and emotionally.

Most of us don't think about these five layers, and as a result we cannot see how they are working and supporting one another. For instance, our minds can be hijacked through the seduction of comparison. Or, we may not be treating our bodies with care and consideration when we grapple with addictions, lack of movement, or body shaming. These kinds of life-depleting moments can impact all of the koshas and create unnecessary suffering for you. By bringing awareness to the koshas, and taking time to tend to each of them, you can start to live in greater alignment and integrity with your authentic self.

What's more, even when you find yourself in alignment, it's not a fixed state. Life itself is movement; it is a dance of coming in and out of various states, including alignment. The challenge is to recognize all the moments when you are out of alignment, and be kind to yourself while you bring yourself back using the one degree inquiries.

By strengthening each kosha, you will be able to see how each influences the others, leading to a greater understanding of your authentic self—when you change one thing, it can change everything.

The Physical Body

Your physical body is the outer layer of self, and the daily choices you make have real impact on its health and wellness. In order to cultivate a strong relationship with your physical body you are invited to think about what you feed it, how you move it, and how you allow it to experience all of life's possibilities through your senses.

Your body is dense matter which needs to be tended to like a precious garden. The peril is that the body is programmed for survival, and it's an expert at keeping its bones, muscles, organs, and cells working even when it's not receiving the proper support. While warning signs might not show up immediately, many people are functioning below their peak abilities and don't even know it. They think having low energy, mental fog, and mild depression is simply a part of daily life or the natural process of aging. When you start to shift your nutrition, incorporate movement, take time out to recharge, and care for your physical body, everything begins to work more efficiently and you have the potential to source more energy, positive moods, and internal vitality.

On the other end of the spectrum, many people have become overly concerned, or even obsessed, with their physical body. They focus only on what their bodies can do, buckle under societal pressures to look a certain way, wrap their whole worth in the outer features of their physical form, and forget about the other koshas. They live wholly in the physical realm and don't take time to breathe consciously, think with greater clarity, step back and witness what is truly going on.

ONE DEGREE SHIFT INQUIRY:
Your Physical Body

The following suggestions will help you become more in tune with your physical body:

Let's look at your morning routine. Does it make you feel grounded and ready for the day? If not, consider adding these to your morning rituals and creating a new practice. This practice is inspired by Ayurveda, the sister science to yoga.

• Wake up and expose your eyes to natural light to align with the rhythm of nature.

- Scrape your tongue with a tongue scraper before you brush your teeth.
- Drink a glass of warm water—you might consider adding lemon, fennel seeds, or drinking herbal tea in a rotation which can help aid in elimination and digestive health.
- Do fifteen minutes of morning yoga or some kind of gentle movement such as walking or dancing.
- Do five minutes of breathing exercises (see p. 73 for instructions).
- Self-massage with loving affirmations.
- Do five minutes of the "I Welcome Meditation" (see p. 56), or just sit quietly with your thoughts.
- Read something inspirational or uplifting.
- Journal and set intentions for the day.

Here are some questions that may also lead to a one degree shift. You don't need to address them all—small shifts lead to big changes over time.

- What are you allowing into your physical body on a daily basis? Is there something that is a crime against wisdom? If so, what is a small shift you could make today?
- What are you looking at and listening to? Does it make you feel more alive? If not, what is a small shift you could make today?
- Is your body in a constant state of stress and strain, or do you carve out space for relaxation? How do you

relax or refuel? What is one thing you could do today to create space for relaxation?

- How many hours are you sleeping? What is your bed-time ritual? What shifts could you make to transform your bedroom into a sacred space? For example, you might commit to setting a certain bedtime, eliminating technology or phones from your room, or diffusing essential oils to help aid in a restful night's sleep.

- Who do you hang out with? Do they feed you or drain you? What boundaries do you need to create with friends or family so you can continue to feel supported?

- What self-care rituals do you incorporate on a weekly basis?

ONE DEGREE SHIFT INQUIRY:
On the Mat Inquiry

One of my favorite sayings is, "How you do anything is how you do everything." And one of the gifts of yoga on the mat is that you can practice how you want to live off the mat! If you're interested in playing with this experiment of shifting parts of your authentic self or your personality that aren't serving you anymore, a place to begin might be as simple as trying a different type of yoga class. For instance, if you love vinyasa, try a restorative yoga class. If you're really tense on the yoga mat and you skip out on the relaxation part, it may be a signal for you to look at where else in your life you are really tense and forgetting to relax. Or, you might find that you're not comfortable slowing down the flow during class. You can investigate where else you are not comfortable slowing down, whether it's the way you speak or how you make decisions. By noticing these comparisons you can start to see them in lots of different places in your life. Self-reflection is a small shift in and of itself.

Another experiment to explore your connection to your physical body might be as simple and powerful as noticing how you stand. How you stand could be a reflection of how you stand in life, which is why shifting your posture could be a powerful small shift to investigate. Try this experiment and see how holding an aligned *tadasana*, or mountain pose, makes you feel. First read through the instructions, then allow yourself to try it on. Taking the time simply to stand, breathe, bring awareness to the moment, and experience the feeling could be powerful enough.

- Standing tall, place your feet hip-width distance apart and parallel, pointing straight forward. Lift and spread your toes, then lay them softly down on the floor. Rock back and forth and side to side. Press down through the soles of your feet by distributing your weight evenly between the inner and outer edges, the ball of each foot, and your heels.

- Allow a very slight bend in your knees. Imagine you were squeezing a yoga block between your thighs to awaken the inner thigh muscles.
- Keeping a natural curve in the lower back, lift your ribs up, away from your hips, keeping length in both the belly and lower back. Lift your chest and heart toward the ceiling.
- Relax your shoulders and reach your fingertips toward the ground.
- Press the crown of your head upward, lengthening your neck.
- Find a soft smile on the face. Jaw is relaxed. Find space between the eyebrows. Release stress and tension.
- Take three deep breaths in and out through your nose, and release the posture.
- Notice how you feel. See how often you can incorporate *tadasana* throughout the day. How does taking time to stand in alignment impact how you feel and how you engage with the moment?

The Breath Body

The breath, the wind of life, is an unseen energetic force. The breath body is a constant reminder of your shared experience with everything that is alive on the planet. It also points to the power of cycles which exist in you and all around you. The first thing you did when you came out of the womb was take a breath, and the last thing you do before you pass will be your final exhale. In some ways every breath in is an opportunity to begin again or start fresh, and with every exhale we practice letting go and releasing.

Most people don't ever pause to contemplate their breath and how having a relationship with it can be a true game changer. Since the breath relates to energy you can think about it like a storage house that registers many of your life experiences. In particular, if you go through trauma—whether physical, mental, or emotional—stagnation can build up and restrict the full movement of your breath. If you imagine your breath traveling through internal rivers, when you experience challenge—and sweep it under the rug without some sort of integration—dams start to amass, restricting the flow of vital energy. In this way the breath layer is truly a bridge between body and mind, so when you build a relationship to it you are better able to support the other facets of your life experience.

ONE DEGREE SHIFT INQUIRY:
The Breath Body

The complete yogic breath or three-part breath is a conscious breath that utilizes your full lung capacity. It has the potential to calm the mind and enhance inward focus, and it is an invitation to a more intimate experience with the present moment.

Instructions for three-part breathing:

- Sit or lay down in a comfortable position. If you are sitting, sit tall with an elongated spine and your belly relaxed.
- Close your mouth and relax your jaw, and release any tension in your face.
- Allow your lips to gently touch and breathe slowly in

and out through your nose. If you are congested you can breathe through the mouth, just let it be a slower breath; imagine you are breathing air through a straw.

- Rest your hands on your belly. As you inhale, imagine your belly as a balloon that is inflating as much as possible. Exhale through the nose, let the belly soften again. Continue this until you feel the belly inflating on an inhale and releasing on an exhale.

- Now bring your hands onto the side of the ribs. On your inhale, feel your ribs expand as they press into your hands. On the exhale, feel the ribs release. Repeat several times.

- Next, bring your hands onto your heart and collarbone area. Inhale and feel the heart area lift, exhale as the chest softens and releases. Repeat several times.

- Finally, combine all three of the parts on the inhale. Inhale and imagine your belly inflating like a balloon, ribs expanding, breath moving all the way into the collarbones or the heart to make a complete inhalation.

- Release the chest, ribs, and belly as you make a complete exhalation.

- Let the inhalation and exhalation be as slow as feels comfortable.

- Continue this breathing pattern for ten inhales and ten exhales.

- Release the breath practice and observe the effects of three-part breathing. Has anything shifted? What do you notice? How do you feel?

The Mental Body

There are different qualities to the mind and often it can feel like it gets split in two: an empowered mind (sometimes people refer to it as a *higher mind*; however, this to me makes it feel like one is *good* and one is *bad*—and my aim is to stay away from this feeling), and a critical mind. Your empowered mind has the ability to imagine infinite possibilities and dreams, shift perspectives when long-standing beliefs are no longer useful, and recognize the beliefs that can be uplifting. It allows you to feel your emotions without creating stories or justifications that are untrue. The critical mind is a gremlin, a part of you that holds on to fears. It can self-sabotage, be unnecessarily judgmental, and avoids change. The critical mind is not a personality flaw, and is a very natural part of our evolutionary makeup that allows us to second-guess our decisions so we can make more discerning choices.

The aim for the mental body is to find a healthy relationship with our empowered mind so we can recognize the thoughts that support creativity and innovative thinking, as well as recognize the negative thoughts from the critical mind that appear when we are self-sabotaging.

Sometimes, our critical mind can hijack a situation and create distress by holding on to limiting beliefs and false perceptions: the distortions. When you find yourself using words like "I can't," "should," or "realistic," it's a good indication that the gremlin is lurking around and suppressing your empowered mind. Think of the last time you planned on meditating five mornings a week for the next month or intended to create some kind of new habit—what happened? Usually, despite your best intentions, something gets in the way, and you hear yourself thinking, "Do you really want to get up early to meditate?" And the next thing you know you've hit the snooze button. Or you may realize that it's time to quit a job or leave a relationship, yet every time you try, all of the rationalizations to stay come rushing in and convince you why you shouldn't change the status quo.

One time when I was teaching in New York City I decided to run an experiment. As I was walking down a busy avenue I took twenty minutes to think kind thoughts about every person I walked past. Then, for twenty minutes I walked by people judging them, allowing my mind to latch onto any perceived and imaginary imperfection. The shift in my feeling state was palpable. The first round felt so much more connected, kind, and compassionate—the world I imagine I want to be a part of. The second round felt troubling, even shocking, because it was so easy to switch into a critical mind-set and shield my heart. The truth is that both perspectives are always available to us, and it is such a subtle yet potent shift from one to the other. As you go through your day-to-day life, you are basically running this same experiment all the time—but unconsciously. Part of the practice of coming into greater authenticity and alignment is learning to create a boundary with the gremlin self and choosing to let your empowered mind view the world. When you do, you will start to experience yourself with fresh eyes that allow access to greater joy, freedom, ease, and connection.

If your thoughts have such an influential role on how beliefs are formed, imagine what they are doing to your emotional circuitry? When we continue to have repetitive unhelpful thoughts, it's almost like we create a groove in the mind and we get stuck on a thought. When you get stuck, it can become much more challenging to see clearly and act from a place of sober empowerment which then can have an impact on your perceptions, decisions, and emotions.

ONE DEGREE SHIFT INQUIRY:
The Mental Body

Journal, create a work of art, or record yourself speaking, moving, or dancing as if your empowered mind is fully expressed. Once you can see what your empowered mind says, looks, and acts like, try any (or all) of the following experiments:

- Spend one full day using your empowered mind. How do you speak to others? How would you engage with others? What would you need to be aware of to live from this place more often? What do you need to say to your gremlin for this to happen? Journal about the experience.
- For three days, any time you need to make a decision, ask your empowered mind to make it. Journal about the experience. It may be useful to have a physical reminder during this exercise to remind yourself to ask your empowered mind to answer, such as wearing a rubber band on your wrist or a specific piece of jewelry.
- Let your empowered mind have a conversation with your gremlin. What would they say to each other? Allow yourself to just observe the conversation without judgment. Journal about the experience.

The Witness Body

The fourth kosha is all about sourcing inner wisdom, insight, and greater reflection. It is the part of yourself that lovingly "sees." This is the ability to observe your decisions without judgment; to become a compassionate observer who knows, chooses, and discriminates between choices that will be life enhancing and those that detract from your vital energy. When you are in a relationship with the mental and emotional parts of your life you are better able to create space, step back, and witness what is going on. By watching first and not immediately reacting, you provide an opportunity for your inner voice to shine through.

ONE DEGREE SHIFT INQUIRY:
Strengthening the Witness: Awareness with Compassion

- Take a comfortable position, either seated or lying down.
- Begin by taking three clearing breaths—deep breath in, then a big exhale with a sigh.
- Allow yourself to simply begin to notice whatever it is that you notice. Become aware of the experience that you are having, welcoming everything in with compassion; simply notice—this is the key to this practice!
- You might begin with your physical body—what do you notice? What are you aware of?
- Say to yourself: "I notice" or "I am aware of X." You might say, "I notice a tightness in my shoulders," or "I am aware I have a full belly," or "I notice my breath."
- Set a timer, and for the next five minutes go on a "noticing with compassion" journey—simply saying to yourself whatever it is you notice.

• After you have completed this, journal your thoughts. What did you take away from this experience? What is the power of noticing or having awareness? How could this support you being more authentically yourself?

The Bliss Body

The bliss body pulsates at the core of our being while at the same time permeating all the other planes of our existence. It is the eternal center of consciousness, which is woven into the primal instincts and structural components of our body. Some people might call this the universe or nature; some might call it God, Goddess, or consciousness; the understanding that there's more going on than just ourselves. When we have that understanding, we experience a sweet sense of interconnectedness. This feeling of being plugged in is always available to you, yet so many are not tending to their other layers so they can't experience that which is right before their eyes.

When you take time to do things that nourish your physical body, make space for a relationship with your breath, step back to observe the inner dialogue of thought, and practice rituals to enhance awareness, you will be able to see more, listen, and take actions which support you to feel more connected, and as a result experience more blisslike moments. This might show up as unstoppable laughter, savoring the company of a child or another person you deeply love, delighting in a first bite of food, getting lost in the brilliance of a flower, losing the sense of time while creating art, being in nature or in the midst of an intimate connection.

ONE DEGREE SHIFT INQUIRY:
Opening the Bliss Body

By taking time to tend to the other layers, you are more likely to be open to the sweet and blissful moments around you. And when you take time to ask yourself the simple question, "Where is bliss?" it reminds you that bliss is all around. When you can remember that, you have the ability to access the bliss body more often—the interconnectedness of us all.

- Place your attention on some aspect of nature and ask yourself, "Where is the bliss in this scenery?"
- Place your attention on your closest friend, and ask yourself, "Where is the bliss in this relationship?"
- Place your attention on someone you may be in conflict with and ask yourself, "Where is the bliss now, even though the relationship is not perfect?"

Allow yourself to dive into this inquiry with as many different parameters as you can. Though your gremlins might try to jump in and block you from seeing bliss, with practice, you might be able to create a boundary with your gremlins and begin to see bliss all around.

ONE DEGREE SHIFT INQUIRY:
The Kosha Inquiry

Write down how you have experienced a specific kosha. It might be recognition of a challenging situation or a more easeful experience. Some examples include:

The Kosha	Sample Entry	Your Entry
Physical	Knee injury, rock climbing, hiking, sex, eating a food and noticing its effects	
Breath	Being held underwater by a wave and coming up for a breath, taking a deep breath to sing another note in a song	
Mental	Ruminating thoughts after a breakup or job loss, creative brainstorming about a new idea	
Witness	Recognizing how a part of your body feels during a yoga class, pausing before you respond in an argument and listening first	
Bliss	Being in awe while visiting a nature spot, feeling free on the dance floor, noticing a connection when someone listens to you	

The Ultimate Mystery of Authenticity

The search for authenticity can invite you in to the ultimate mystery of walking the path of yoga. It asks you to delve deep into the inquiry of both the earthly experience of who you really are now, who you were before your grandparents were born, and who you will be after you take your final breath. "Is there a part of me that has always existed and always will?" "Is there a place inside of me, an essence that is infinite and interwoven into the eternal fabric of existence?"

These questions invite you deep into the inquiry of yoga which invites you to look for a place where you feel eternal, whole, and complete. You can be inspired by many teachers, sacred texts, or even this book, and at the end of the day you are the only one who can walk your path and discover these answers for yourself. Just asking these questions can provide a release, the contented feeling of at-home-ness and easeful-ness while you honor the great mystery, knowing that your journey is a continuum. You are a part of something bigger than yourself.

For me, this quest creates the feeling that I'm always at home, no matter where I go. No matter what I experience. And while there will be moments when I forget that I am part of this great mystery, there are also moments when I remember. And in those moments of remembering, I can take a deep exhale and know that everything is okay.

I want to know myself completely.
I want to speak radical truth.
I want to have clear boundaries with no need for armor.
I want to be responsible for my impact.
I want to relax when I take it all too seriously.

I want to be there when others can't.
I want to love when it seems hard.
I want to forgive when it seems impossible.
I want to use my words as a source of integrity and kindness.
I want to honor those who have come before me.
I want to treat the earth with respect.
I want to grow into the me that is patiently waiting.

Accountability and Integrity

You have the power to choose which part of
yourself you want to be in charge.
The empowered self, awakened self, future self, the gremlin self.
The millions of selves that all live inside you.
Be quiet enough to notice.
Be brave enough to make a change.
Be strong enough to keep it that way.
Be kind enough to all the parts of you.

⁓

Even if you have the courage to ask, "Who am I really?" most likely the best version of yourself isn't going to show up every single time. There will be moments, sometimes even daily, where you find yourself out of alignment. There will be times when even with the best intentions, you can be caught unaware and make a decision that unintentionally negatively affects someone else, or puts you on a path that doesn't feel aligned. This could be how you respond in a conversation, or by staying in a relationship that doesn't serve you, or making lifestyle choices that aren't nourishing. This is how small choices or major decisions can affect your life.

The key is knowing that messes, mishaps, and mistakes will happen, yet you have to clean up your misalignments, whether in the moment or when you realize it in hindsight. This level of responsibility is known as accountability. And just like becoming more aligned with your authentic self, becoming more accountable can take practice.

Self-reflection is essential for accountability. That doesn't mean you always have to apologize or take the blame. It means you have to dare to look at what's happened, and have the willingness to take responsibility for your actions that may have hurt yourself or someone else. There are consequences to all the choices you make—in every moment of every day, you are having an impact. Think of it like this: What if every day on your way to work you passed a stop sign, and each time you decided to drive right through it? Now, the odds are that most times nothing will happen, yet eventually, you're probably going to get hurt or hurt somebody else.

When you acknowledge that there are consequences to your choices, you start to realize that you are a co-creator of your reality. You can influence the outcome of each and every day. And while there are no guarantees in life—we can't predict the future or be in control of everything—we can choose a path or actions that are likely to produce the most desirable results.

When you are accountable for your actions, you realize one of the few things you are in control of is your own integrity: the ability to be your authentic self, most of the time, and to be accountable for the moments when you are not.

Yoga teaches that integrity increases our probability of success as we attempt to skillfully navigate the world. The aspiration is to raise the bar to an even higher level, what one of my teachers, Lonny Jarrett, refers to as uncommon integrity. My friend and yoga educator Danny Arguetty is an example of someone who has uncommon integrity. His choices are thoughtful and reflect his strong feelings about the environment and how we could be treating each other. For example, he sold his car and rides his bike or uses public transportation to get to work every day for the sake of being responsible for his carbon footprint. He knows the negative impacts of destroying virgin forests so he uses minimal paper products or makes sure to buy recycled paper goods whenever he can. He researches every company before he buys something, looking for the most sustainable and socially responsible brands. The companies he invests in are the companies he believes in, not just the ones that are the most likely to turn a profit. Sometimes this isn't the easiest life, but he is committed to holding himself accountable to the highest standard he has set for himself.

Uncommon integrity does not mean you need to be perfect; it is simply calling yourself forth and raising the bar on your impact. We all need to decide for ourselves what uncommon integrity can look like. Other examples might include raising the bar on communication by forgoing gossiping or decreasing complaining. Or, it might be putting your phone away when you are in the company of others so you can be more present with them.

ONE DEGREE SHIFT INQUIRY:
Set a Baseline for Accountability

This chapter invites you into the experiment of revealing the ways you can be more accountable with yourself and with others. The first one degree shift inquiry regarding accountability is setting a baseline, where you are right now:

- What does integrity mean for you?
- Where do you immediately see areas in which you need to be accountable for your actions?

Your interests or the way your life is structured might not be the same as Danny's, and yet you have the capacity to have uncommon integrity toward what it is you deem to have high value.

- What do you care deeply about that you would raise your bar toward uncommon integrity?
- What is one small shift you can make today to start living this way?

Accountability Can Begin at the Beginning

I believe that before we look at how we treat others, there is value in investigating our relationship with ourselves. From a yogic perspective, the body is comprised of energetic pathways called *nadis*, which means channels or streams. When these channels are open your internal energy is flowing unencumbered, and you can more easily align to your authentic self. However we don't, and cannot expect to, live with a perfect internal flow all the time. Sometimes disturbances occur that literally block the stream and create a dam, and when this happens, we are less likely to be the most empowered version of ourselves. When you feel like you are stuck in the riptide of life, when you feel like you are reacting instead of responding, when you feel overwhelmed, frustrated, or disappointed on a regular basis, these might be indicators that your channels are blocked.

There are many ways these channels can be impacted, but for many of us, these blockages stem from childhood. They could have occurred after a traumatic event we didn't know how to make sense of or that we didn't get the opportunity to integrate; or they could even be small, cumulative losses or disappointments. These dams can impact our mental body and powerfully contribute to our developing personality. We then make choices that align with our personality that might not serve us well, because we are seeing the world through distorted lenses.

For instance, if a child grows up with a violent parent, that child may create a perception that the world is not a safe place, in or outside their home. This distortion may influence the child's behavior, and as they get older there is the potential to make choices that are not aligned with their authentic self. Some people might develop a strong resiliency, while others may let people take advantage of them rather than advocating for what they need. Over time, the mental body can become a warehouse for this false reality, and we collect data that confirms our behaviors and beliefs. As a consequence, we are prevented from skillfully riding the waves, the ups and downs of life, because our personality traits compensate for our inability to see what is really happening: this is how we can keep getting stuck. This feels like we are being pulled by a riptide—and we do not know how to get out.

Part of the practice of living yoga is recognizing when these energetic rivers are not flowing—and then putting ourselves into different experiments to open the dams so they can flow freely again. The way to do this is to alter the mental body so that you can begin to see beyond your stories, beyond your wounds, and beyond your fears. Once you do, you can break down the habits that have been holding you back so that you can more consciously live in the world with integrity.

Later in the book, you will explore your story and the ways it impacts your personality and the way you interact with the world. For now, sit with the idea that we all have a story, and yours may be impacting you more than you realize. What's more, when you are acting out of alignment, the decisions you make based on your story might be impacting others as well. In order to be accountable, you're invited to lovingly reflect on your story and the way it has shaped who you are today. And then, begin to make more choices that are in alignment with your authentic self.

Forgive Yourself

One place where you could begin to become more accountable might be forgiving yourself for moments of misalignment. Most likely you were wearing various masks and hiding your authentic self because you were acting from a place of unresolved historical imprints. Many people have shame or guilt about their past behaviors and are unable to forgive themselves. The truth is, you are just now learning about what it means to be living as your most authentic self. Ultimately, we would all benefit from being kind to one another and ourselves, because believe it or not, we are all doing the best that we can as we learn to ride the waves.

When you have acted out of alignment, there are consequences.

When you truly understand the impact you had and make a sincere effort to clean up your mess and choose differently moving forward, it is much easier to forgive yourself.

ONE DEGREE SHIFT INQUIRY:
Forgiveness Letter to Yourself

Take a moment and ask yourself if there is something you need to forgive yourself for.

- Where in your life have you acted out of alignment and impacted yourself or others in ways that were unintended and potentially hurtful, or in a way you are not proud of?
- What would become available if you let go of guilt and shame of past behaviors?

Then, write yourself a letter completing each of the following prompts:
  Dear *your name* ...

- I forgive you for...
- What I learned from this experience was...
- I can promise I will not repeat this behavior again because I now know...
- And if I do repeat this behavior I will rectify it by...
- With this commitment I will now be able to...

Stop Harming Yourself

I have a friend who's a cutter. She's not trying to kill herself, but she does harm herself when she takes a razor blade and cuts her arms or legs. Most of us don't cut ourselves externally, but we do cut ourselves internally by shaming ourselves, or by letting our gremlin, the critical mind, run an internal negative dialogue. We can judge ourselves, criticize ourselves, and compare ourselves to others. Maybe you're saying things to yourself that are not loving or kind; maybe you're judging your body or your actions or your history.

Part of the practice of learning how to become accountable is to explore how you can stop harming yourself and start loving yourself instead. Take a moment to notice the ways you are harming yourself internally. Are there ways in which you are breaking your own heart by acting without integrity? What is it that you are actually wanting, and what is the void that you are trying to fill when you are committing these crimes against wisdom?

Creating a boundary with your gremlin is one way you can stop harming yourself. When you feel stuck or less than, take a minute to ask yourself what Katie Brauer says: "Who is driving the bus of your life?" If it's one of your gremlins, notice how long it's been in charge, and what the consequences are of allowing it to keep deciding which direction you are heading.

If you do decide to create a boundary, you don't need to yank the gremlin out of the front seat, as there are gentler ways—you can relate to it kindly and assertively. For instance, if the gremlin of obsessiveness is visiting, remember that if channeled skillfully, this same energy could show up as dedication or devotion.

You can also create a safe space for your gremlin to speak for two minutes, giving it the opportunity to fully express itself. This will often reduce your gremlin's power and hold, because when we have an internal thought that keeps expressing itself and we don't give it an outlet (expressing it physically with your body, journaling, sharing it with a friend), it can become more powerful in its vacuum. Yet when we can experience the thought aloud, we can hear how dissonant it really is, and we can get past it (at least for a bit).

Ask yourself the following questions:

- What are the ways your gremlin thinks that it is protecting you?
- What does a boundary look like with your gremlin?
- What does your empowered mind have to say to your gremlin?

The "Be Nice" Inquiry

Try this practice for the next seven days: only say nice things about yourself (this includes your thoughts). To be clearer—stop saying sh*tty things about yourself to yourself, or to others.

The Octopus on Your Face

A blind spot is an aspect of yourself that you cannot see, or that you refuse to see. Blind spots can be both positive and not so positive traits, behaviors, or ways of interacting with the world. And they can range from being innocuous to having quite a harmful impact on yourself and others. I like to think of a blind spot like an octopus stuck on your face: you don't even see it, but everyone else does.

We all have blind spots, and when we are interested in exploring accountability, we can be open to receiving feedback from those we respect. We need each other in order to learn and grow. Every interaction with others is an opportunity to become more accountable for who you are, and who you want to evolve into. It might not feel so great when someone fills you in on your blind spots, and if you allow your defenses to soften, that feedback could shift your life one degree for the better.

A few years back, I threw myself a birthday gathering with some of my closest friends. I asked each of them to come prepared to tell me what they saw as my blind spot. Now I realize that for many, this doesn't sound like a good time, but for me it was one of the best gifts I ever received. It was an opportunity for me to gather data. Some of the things that were shared didn't resonate, and some I immediately felt resistance to, and realized they were where I needed to place my attention. One of my biggest blind spots that was shared was whenever I accomplished something worthy of celebrating, I would brush if off and move on to the next thing without honoring my accomplishment. For example, when I received my master's degree, I didn't even tell anyone. One quality I admire in others is humility, so my value of humility was actually standing in the way of celebrating and honoring my dedication and hard work.

Some of my friends also felt that I don't prioritize their friendship because I don't always respond to texts or phone calls immediately. The reality for me is that I choose not to carry my phone most of the time, and try to live my life as technology free as I possibly can. What I didn't realize was that my actions were creating a feeling among my friends that I didn't care about them, which certainly was not my intention.

When I investigated what they were saying, it led me to take responsibility for areas of my life I needed to clean up, including these friendships. When I dug deeper, I wondered if there was another reason besides how I value humility or my time offline. Is it also possible that while I value humility or privacy, I also have a discomfort being the center of attention—an unconscious wall I was putting up in my friendships? Without knowing it, my blind spots were limiting my ability to be in alignment with my authentic self. Now that I know what these blind spots are, I can become more accountable, and make addressing them part of my regular practice. By doing so, I can be more aware of how I impact myself and others.

ONE DEGREE SHIFT INQUIRY:
Blind Spots

Ask five people to share the positive traits they see in you, as well as areas of potential improvement (you are just collecting data, so don't assign a value to this feedback yet). Then, ask them what they think you don't realize about yourself: your blind spots. Journal about what they say, and also your response to their feedback. Then, record below any of the blind spots you receive from more than one person.

Now, think about what you have learned about yourself. What small shift can you make today to be in a healthier relationship with your blind spots?

Blind spot	What you learned	What small shift can you make?
I.		
2.		

3.		
4.		
5.		

Learn from the People You Trigger

Some would consider me an outgoing and outspoken person. Others might see these same traits negatively, as being domineering and opinionated. Clearly, not everyone is going to resonate with my personality and me, and the same is true for you. Part of walking the path of yoga is having the courage to be accountable for your authenticity, because when you are aligned with who you really are, you have the potential to influence someone else to do the same. You don't need to water down who you are, and you are invited to recognize that you impact others. Be conscientious of the parts of you others might find triggering—for the sake of your contribution to the world around you, and all of your relationships.

I once took a life-coaching workshop, and during a bathroom break I noticed a woman from the training standing in the hallway crying. When I checked in with her, she told me that I made her upset by the way I was taking up space during our group discussion. Then she told me I reminded her of her childhood best friend who was always getting all the attention. I didn't really know how to respond, so I reached out to the teacher to ask for advice. The teacher reminded me that there is enough space for everyone to be who they are.

I could have easily said, "Well, that is just her issue," or I could have gone the other way and beat myself up for being too assertive. So while I know that not everybody is going to like me, I can take responsibility and practice the art of tolerating the consequences of being myself. The complexity of walking the path of accountability is that you have permission to be fully your authentic self, which means there will be moments where you might trigger people. The challenge is to accept yourself where you are because you are perfect and complete, and also recognize that you are evolving and there is always room for change.

So I had to ask myself the following questions:

- What if everything she said was true? If so, what can I learn about myself?
- What if none of what she said was true? Then how could I honor myself?
- What if some of what she said was true? How do I balance the learning and the honoring?

Learn from the People Who Trigger You

Yoga teaches that the person who triggers you, or gets under your skin, can actually be offering you a valuable lesson. You don't need to like this person; you don't need to have this person in your life; and it is worth looking to figure out why you are getting so activated. How is this person a reflection of something for you to look at in yourself? For example, when I did my first yoga teacher training, there was a woman in my training who triggered me. Anytime our teacher asked a question, this woman would raise her hand and snap her fingers to try to get the teacher's attention. I found her actions to be annoying and I thought, "If only she wasn't here, this would be the best training ever."

Where in your life are you repeating similar words? "If only this person wasn't my boss," or "If only this person wasn't my neighbor," or "If only this person wasn't my mother-in-law, or my sister."

At the time, I was working with my mentor, Patrick, and I remember asking him, "Can't people just be annoying and it has nothing to do with me? If you met this lady, you would see how irritating she actually is." To my dismay, he told me, "No, it has everything to do with you. There's a reason you're triggered by this woman."

I didn't want to believe him. I continued to seek validation that my feeling didn't have anything to do with me, so I reached out to one of my friends in the training and asked her, "Isn't that girl so annoying?" My friend asked, "Who are you talking about?" I couldn't believe it. "What do you mean, who am I talking about? The annoying girl!" My friend hadn't noticed her at all, because what was being triggered in me was my wound to heal, not my friend's.

After reflecting on these two conversations I decided to take this conundrum on as an inquiry. I started to unpack why this woman annoyed me so much. When I thought more about her potential motivations, I imagined she was simply looking for attention. She wanted to be seen. She wanted to be validated. And when I recognized this, my feelings about her started to shift.

This led me to a whole slew of contemplations around where in my life I didn't feel seen, or recognized, and where I was looking for attention. Though my actions were not similar to hers, there was a similar energy needing to be healed—the little girl inside me who wanted to be seen, accepted, and genuinely loved. Maybe that's why I'm outgoing and outspoken. Or when my gremlin is driving the bus, I can come across as domineering and opinionated. I learned from this experience that no matter where we go in life, most likely there will be someone who will trigger us until we figure out what is trying to get our attention.

It's quite natural to respond to people who trigger you the same way I responded to this woman: "She annoys me; I'm nothing like her." But what if you turned that reflexive response on its head, and instead of dismissing that person, thought about why you were triggered: Do you see any similarity between you and that person? Or, is the behavior that's triggering you actually something you aspire toward?

Most people are actually doing the best they can, *and* they have wounds, stories, and places where they do not feel totally aligned, just like you. We are all perfect and at the same time evolving into our different perfection. The process of becoming more accountable is ongoing, and the practice is in remembering we are all in it together.

ONE DEGREE SHIFT INQUIRY:
Is the Person Who Gets Under Your Skin Your Teacher?

It takes a certain level of curiosity to be able to navigate interactions with others and learn from them. Douglas Brooks, a scholar of Hinduism, shares a unique expression that I think can be a useful way of unpacking and learning from people who trigger you: "I'm nothing like you, I'm something like you, I'm nothing but you."

What would shift for you if instead of just writing triggers off, you took time to contemplate how they might hold an insight, a gem for you to learn more about yourself and the world around you?

- Who triggers you?
- How are you something like them?
- How are you nothing like them?

- How are you nothing but them?
- Is there something about them that you actually aspire toward?
- What are they teaching you?

Your Energetic Impact

Another place to look at how to be more accountable is getting a better understanding of your energetic impact. As soon as you enter a room, you have an impact on the space and the people in it, even before you know anything about them or before they know anything about you. The way you stand, breathe, talk, dress, all has an impact energetically. Whether you know it or not, you are already establishing a relationship in those first moments.

We can all become more curious and accountable regarding our energetic impact. In reality, what you think your energetic impact is, what you want your impact to be, and what your impact actually is, might be three very different things. For instance, you might think you are charming and draw people toward you with your friendly nature, and you wish your impact was to make people feel included. However, others may see you as manipulative, which can actually push people away if they sense that your friendliness has an agenda, or you have an ulterior motive.

Here's a short list of energetic vibrations that can impact others. Interestingly, each of these can be perceived in two different ways: the "light," and the "shadow." You can think of the light and shadow like the sun and the moon—one is not better than the other. Shadows form when something gets in the way of the light, but the light is still present. So rather than thinking about shadows as bad or negative, think about them this way: What is the obstacle in the way of the light that we can tend to?

Recognizing the qualities you possess and the energy you give off can help you be more accountable and be more adept at navigating life. Usually we have a dominant energy (or two). The most dominant is likely related to your authentic self. You may have also been influenced by a personality trait you took on to compensate for the dams that were created along the way. In each of the following types of energies, the first is the light, the second is the shadow:

- Assertive/Aggressive
- Charming/Manipulative
- Effervescent/Flighty
- Enigmatic/Dangerous
- Lighthearted/Aloof
- Nurturing/Weak
- Wise/Know-It-All

ONE DEGREE SHIFT INQUIRY:
Connecting with Your Energetic Impact

- Can you think of someone who embodies either the light or shadow of each energy type?
- What about you points toward an energy type? What energy type do you imagine someone who just met you might say you embody?
- What are the ways in which you are channeling the light side of this energy and the shadow side?
- How might you work with this energy and become more skillful? With yourself? With others?

Sometimes we are triggered by people who have similar energies to us, because on an unconscious level there is either a feeling of competing for space or you see the shadow side of yourself in them. Other times we can be triggered by people who have a very different energy type from us, because either we simply don't understand them or they possess a quality we wish we had more of.

- Who are you drawn to? What qualities do they possess that you are wanting to expand in yourself?
- Who pushes you away? Is there a quality they possess that you actually wish you had more of?
- Is there a blind spot in which you demonstrate a similar energy? Though the behavior or actions might not be the same, in what area are you the same as this person?

Conscious Communication: Words Matter

If we go back to the idea that authenticity is aligning what you say, think, feel, and do, becoming accountable with what you say is an important step on the path of living yoga. The truth is, words have significant power: they can uplift and inspire or they can be hurtful and cut people down. The conscious use of language helps us take responsibility for how we feel about ourselves, and how we affect others. By becoming aware of the language we use, we can harvest the rewards of honesty, sincerity, and openheartedness.

Conscious communication is an opportunity, as Swami Kripalu says, for asking the question, "Are your words an improvement on silence?" Before I speak, I try to choose my language carefully and ask myself, "What am I saying? Why am I saying it, and is it uplifting? Is it useful?" And most important, "Are my words an improvement upon silence? Am I adding value to the conversation, whether it's online, in person, with what I write, or with what I say in casual conversation?

For instance, I try to speak in the affirmative, focusing on what I want rather than what I don't want. By putting my attention on what I want rather than what isn't working, I can be accountable for cultivating my next evolution instead of being stuck in the past. So often people will say, "I don't want to forget to do that." Instead, I would reframe this by saying, "I want to remember to do that." Instead of saying, "I don't want to get sick," you might say, "I want to stay healthy."

I also try to curb my complaints, because complaining seems to have reached epidemic proportions! Some people are addicted to negativity and love to talk about everything that isn't working in their life, what's broken, and what needs to be fixed. I'm not saying we never need to vent about what is feeling heavy or challenging, just that we'd all benefit if there were a conscious balance between venting and being grateful for what we have.

Part of becoming more accountable is focusing on words that uplift and inspire. If I'm walking a path of yoga and part of my aim is to make a more gentle, friendly, kind world, are my words adding to this gentle, kind, and compassionate world, or are my words adding to a toxic world? One way I try to be conscious of this is by taking the words "good," "bad," "right," and "wrong" out of my vocabulary as often as possible. This prevents me from getting caught up in the labeling of a situation, and instead I can rely on how I feel, and respond to the feeling, rather than the surface label and judgment.

For instance, my grandmother made delicious oatmeal cookies when I was growing up, and I have no idea how many cups of sugar that batter contained, but I am certain it was a lot! Eating those cookies is one of my fondest memories of childhood. Nowadays, most nutritionists and doctors would say that eating an excess of sugar is *bad*. And while there is certainly evidence that eating too much sugar is not supportive of a healthy lifestyle, I'm still grateful when my mother makes these cookies for me now because of the sweet memories I associate them with.

So which belief is right? Is it the science that says sugar is bad for me? Or is it the joyful feeling I experience each year when I eat the cookies and think about my grandmother? The answer is, it depends. Each moment is an opportunity for me to dive in and ask, "What is the most skillful action I can take now in relation to the cookies?" Sometimes, the answer is just to eat the cookies. Other times, the most skillful answer is just to walk away from the cookies. I get to decide and I have to tolerate the consequences of my choices.

Holding this attitude of openness is why I try to say the word "and" rather than saying the word "but" when I'm making a comparison. I'm interested in being able to hold both the shadow and the light of a situation without making one right and the other wrong. To me, using the word "but" often negates whatever is said before it, as in, "I hear what you are saying, but I don't agree." Using the word "and" helps me hold a bigger perspective and to be more accountable to my thoughts, as in, "I hear what you are saying, and I also would like to share X," or "You did a really great job, and next time you could consider X."

When you use the word "but," people often only hear what they didn't do right. The word "and" allows the conversation to stay open and makes the person you are speaking to feel like you heard them. It can allow you to be able to speak and hold your own truth without having to make someone or a situation wrong. It is a more inclusive and collaborative way of speaking and leaves more possibility rather than just shutting someone down.

ONE DEGREE SHIFT INQUIRY:
Conscious Speech Mondays

If yoga is a path of intimacy and the art of becoming intimate with life, a one degree shift can be becoming more intimate, and more conscious, with your words.

Pick a Monday and focus on the words you're choosing:

- Are your words uplifting?
- Are your words true?
- Are your words necessary?
- Do your words focus on the solution rather than the problem?
- How do you own the words you use and become aligned with them?
- Are you saying what you actually mean?

Accountability and the "I" Statement

We live in a world where people often deflect what they are feeling and flip their personal experience onto someone else or onto the group. Have you ever heard someone say, "You know when you start a new job and you're really nervous or you're really afraid that you're not going to fit in or understand the work?" What they are doing is a deflection: they are assuming that what they feel is what everyone is feeling or should be feeling. Most often this is being done unconsciously and in a way, it looks to build consensus, affirmation, and relatedness; it isn't malicious at its core, yet it can create more barriers than connection.

Statements that use words such as "it," "you," "people," or "they," rather than "I" place responsibility on someone or something other than ourselves. Even "we" can be a statement of togetherness (as in "We love each other") or a statement that diffuses or disguises an "I" statement ("We should fix dinner") which tends to crowd out the possibility that the other person might be experiencing something different. Using "the," "this," and "that" when we really mean "my," "mine," or "I" helps us to place our feelings outside of ourselves, as in, "This is a stupid situation," when you may actually think, "I don't understand what's going on."

Instead, talking about what you want in the first person—the "I" statement—is an effective way of owning your truth and becoming more accountable for what you feel. The practice is to be as direct as possible while still keeping an open heart and kind tone. For instance, instead of saying, "When did you get home?" a more honest approach could be, "It was late and I feel hurt that you didn't call me when you got home as we agreed upon."

While some of these shifts in language are extremely minute, they can create positive shifts in our relationships. By having the courage to use speech that is real, clear, and empowered, we show up with more accountability. Over time you might find that you've reduced the drama and interpersonal conflict while meeting more of your needs.

ONE DEGREE SHIFT INQUIRY:
Clean Up Your Mess

Children make messes and run away. Living yoga teaches that part of being human is that you might make a mess, and it is critical to take the time to clean it up.

Cleaning up a mess might mean apologizing for your words or behaviors. Yet what often gets in the way is shame, embarrassment, or pride: the discomforts of knowing you may have made a mistake or acted out of alignment. We can feel like we have to defend our past behaviors even if we realize that they were unintentional or even out of integrity. Instead of being accountable, we might point the finger at the other person, spin a false account of how events unfolded, or take partial responsibility, while still holding on to how we were mistreated by the other person.

The first step in cleaning up your mess is owning your mistakes:

- Is there somewhere in your life that feels like you created a mess?
- Where have you stopped being accountable for your actions?
- Where do you need to be accountable for behavior that didn't produce the results you envisioned or intended?
- Where do you need to be accountable for the moments you acted out of integrity?
- Is there something you did or said to someone for which you need to say you are sorry?
- If so, what are you prepared to do about it? What is one small step you could take today?

Do You Want to Be Right?

I once heard my friend and teacher Holly McCormack say, "Do you want to be right or do you want to be in relationship?" What she meant was that trying always to be right can be a dead-end street: it actually hampers the ability to be in a relationship, and what could potentially come about from that relationship. When we are insistent on being right, the other person is often left without their needs met or not feeling heard.

Have you ever found yourself in a conversation with another person or a group of people about something you're passionate about, or a topic you have a strong conviction about or feel like you are an expert in? Sometimes, our desire to be right or to be heard can bring out the shadow side of our energetic impact if we're not coming from a grounded, authentic, or aligned place. When that happens, it can negatively affect relationships, even if the impact is unintentional. The balance is in finding a way to express yourself as both passionate about what you have to share, and also interested in maintaining the relationship.

For instance, I was recently in a staff meeting and at one point I became really excited about some of the organization's opportunities to grow. My mind was spinning: I had a lot of ideas and as I was sharing my thoughts and feelings, I think I came across as more aggressive than I had planned, and certainly more than I had hoped for when I'm trying to communicate something that I really care about. After the meeting I felt uneasy about the whole situation. Even though the points I made felt *right*, I didn't show up to the group the way that I meant to.

I don't expect myself to be perfect. I do expect myself to clean up my messes and call myself forth to a high standard of integrity. When I got home that night, I sent everyone who was at the meeting an email, trying to own my behavior and clean up my mess. I apologized for my potential impact that may have been too intense and asked if there was anything else they needed from me to feel like the relationship was intact. The next day I felt a sense of peace and ease, and I knew I could let that situation go. I didn't feel the need to hold on to it anymore and was able to forgive myself for not always being 100 percent authentic 100 percent of the time. This situation reminded me of the value of taking time to tend relationships that are of importance to me.

Yet even if you offer a heartfelt apology, there may be times when the other person might not forgive you. That doesn't mean you shouldn't say that you're sorry, because all you can do is take responsibility for your words or actions.

However, if you know you've done something that was really hurtful, you have to learn to sit in the discomfort of the other person's timeline. Not everyone is going to be ready to forgive you when you want forgiveness. It might take someone several months or even years to process their hurt. You may have to get comfortable being uncomfortable with the energetic impact between you and somebody else, and hopefully over time, valuable worthwhile connections will be restored.

ONE DEGREE SHIFT INQUIRY:
Reconciling Differences

Being in a relationship also teaches that you can't have it your way all the time. Many stay rigid in the face of diverse opinions and beliefs. When rigidity arises, it often cuts off our ability to relate. As we discussed earlier, do you want to be right or do you want to be in relationship?

One experiment is to try something new: instead of putting up a fight and insisting that you are right, generate just enough space to agree to disagree, or hold the possibility that maybe your view isn't the only or right one.

- Who is in your life and how are you tending to them?
- What brings you together? What tears you apart?
- What makes you unique within your relationship? What makes you similar?
- Where can you let go of being right and be open to other ways of seeing a situation?
- When have you had to reconcile a difference for the sake of something greater than yourself?
- What was the shift you made, and what was the impact?

I'm Sorry, Forgive Me, Thank You, and I Love You

Yoga teaches us the power of love, gratitude, forgiveness, and responsibility, four values that are universally important. For example, the Hawaiian shamans have a technique called *ho'oponopono*, and they believe it's one of the most valuable practices to learn. They call this the Hawaiian code of forgiveness: I'm sorry, please forgive me, thank you, and I love you.

Ho'oponopono means to make right. The purpose of ho'oponopono is to right the wrongs in someone's life. The process offers an introspective way to align with and clean up our relationships. Below is a simple yet effective technique inspired by ho'oponopono.

ONE DEGREE SHIFT INQUIRY:
I'm Sorry, Forgive Me, Thank You,
and I Love You

You can work through this exercise by repeating this back to yourself, inside your head, out loud, writing in a journal, or simply reflecting on it.

Step 1: I'm sorry. Is there something you are sorry for? Have you caused harm to someone else or even yourself? Imagine this person, and direct the energy toward them or yourself by saying what you are sorry for or feel regret about.

Step 2: Please forgive me. As you think about what you have remorse for, whether it was an action done to yourself or someone else, ask for forgiveness. Connect with the feelings that come up as you ask for forgiveness.

Step 3: Thank you. Enter into a moment of gratitude and say "thank you." You could thank yourself for the courage to forgive yourself, or thank someone else for listening. You might say thank you to your body, to the universe, for life itself.

Step 4: I love you. Say "I love you." You can say it to your body, your breath, your heart, your mind, your family, nature, the universe. You can say "I love you" to the obstacles you face or to the ground you walk on. Step into and feel the power of love by repeating "I love you" over and over again.

If you wanted to be more specific and take this inquiry to the next level with someone you might be out of alignment with, try these steps:

- Think of someone with whom you do not feel in total alignment.
- In your mind's eye, construct a small stage below you. Place that person on the stage.
- Imagine an infinite source of love flowing from a cup above the top of your head, and let the source of love flow down inside your body, fill up your body, and overflow to the person on the stage.
- Afterward, have an imaginary discussion with that person and forgive them, and have them forgive you. Then, watch the person walk off stage, and see them floating away. As they do, cut the energy that connects the two of you.
- See if you can think of this person without feeling any negative emotions. If you do feel negative emotions when you do, then do the process again.

They said, "Nothing matters."
And in some way I wanted to believe it.
For a moment believing this felt easier.
But in my bones I knew that was not my truth.
Even if nothing matters, I still care.

I still want to show up,
and be of service to the collective.
I want my actions to contribute
in a way that adds beauty and kindness to the world around me.
We are the great tapestry,
weaving and looming together.
The world is shifting,
a new season is upon us,
a new garden needs to be planted.
We can either re-create that which came before us,
or be daring to put ourselves into a new experiment.
Collaboration, celebration, cooperation
is not that far away
if enough of us show up, get our inner worlds aligned,
and raise the bar of integrity.

Your Sacred Community

You are held by the great community.
The forest, streams, moss, and soil.
The desert, plants, stars, and sky.
The wind, fire, rocks, and water.
The seen and unseen, the known and unknown.
Those who know you and those waiting to meet you.
Embracing you always.

Even though it may seem like we are more connected than ever because of technology, many people I meet express that they are longing for more authentic, nourishing, real-life person-to-person connections. And even though people have thousands of "friends" and "followers," they can still feel isolated, alone, and disconnected. The truth is, whenever we are interacting on our phones, we are still by ourselves.

I've come to think of social media as anything other than social. The bubble we create around our friends and followers can promote a singular viewpoint of reality, further isolating us from differences in opinions, and placing lots of emphasis on our own perspective as we stop listening to and engaging with others who don't hold the same point of view. We seem to have abandoned looking for common ground. And in the extreme, we may allow our preferences to trump what would serve the greater good.

When I look at the parts of our world that have been grossly affected by our unhealthy choices and our lack of understanding of our interconnectedness—plastics in the oceans killing fish and birds, childhood obesity, a failing public education system, homelessness, or the overwhelming amount of depression and anxiety that people suffer from—it makes me realize how much we need to come together for the sake of more creative, out-of-the-box thinking, so we can take steps to solve these challenges. When we come together and call upon each other's brilliance, we can begin to create solutions that are hopeful, inspiring, and effective.

And, living as if we're not impacting each other isn't serving us individually, either. Our gremlins can seem louder, and we are more likely to live in our heads and create stories that don't serve us, distracting us from the unique gifts we bring to the world. These stories can distort our thinking and can make us feel that we are carrying the weight of the world on our shoulders. Or, we can create a story that we are unlovable or that we don't belong. These thoughts can make us feel like we are stuck in a riptide, or keep us blind to our blind spots.

As we learn to honor our authentic self and our individual journey, we can start to see the power of a greater community, because this is where we can find the support we need to become who we really want to be. We don't have to follow the monastic path in order to find answers to our inquiries, or become the yogini who removes herself from the earthly plane in order to discover a connection beyond the tangible world. In fact, one of the essential aspects of yoga is a sense of togetherness, and includes diving into the deep inquiries of life with others.

Yoga invites you to explore how you balance both individual fulfillment while still making a contribution to a larger community. The truth is, we are social creatures, and we have evolved to depend on one another. And we are impacting each other all the time. So while there is great benefit to learning how to be your authentic self, we would also benefit if we could recognize the systems and solutions we have already created together, and figure out how to evolve them into something even more beautiful, uplifting, and inspiring.

My hope is that you are inspired to find a deeper sense of community, and create new, real-life connections. The idea of community invites us to share our experiences. Though you can find value and power in online platforms, spending time with others, in person, is incomparable. One of my aims as an educator is to bring people together in real life, to share experiences, to be in conversation, to grow collectively. I have found that the transformative power of yoga occurs when people come together and support each other in their individual evolution as they dare to be their authentic selves.

Being together in a physical community invites us to learn how to better connect with other people, and honor what we have in common as well as witness our differences. I am not interested in creating a mythic utopia where everyone gets along all the time. Instead, true community can occur when we care for one another, and dare to do better than those who came before us as we blossom into our collective greatest potential.

Every community has the potential to show us that we are never really alone: we are each a single thread, always weaving and looming the tapestry of life together. Life is a collective, an interworking of structures and systems. We see it in our bodies, in the natural world, and in the way our planet, solar system, and universe work. For instance, every cell in your body develops individually, and collectively it develops into the organs that form the community that is you. If one part of your body gets hurt or shuts down, inevitably the rest of your body will have to endure more stress or help you heal.

Community affords time to simply enjoy and savor life's precious moments with others. And more important, when we lean into our community we give others the opportunity to share their unique gifts and talents with us when we need them most, helping us to get out of a riptide or provide different perspectives that can lead to solutions. By leaning into a community you can feel like you are lightening your load, and are less likely to be bogged down by the heaviness of life.

In ashrams, one type of spiritual community, everyone has a specialized role, whether it is to prepare food, clean, be a steward of the land, teach, or run the operations; everyone is there to contribute their part to make the community run with a greater sense of ease and connection. It is not expected for everyone to do everything. Yet in our regular day-to-day life, many of us feel like we have to be a one-person show: taking on all the responsibilities of running a life, like being a parent, partner, worker, cook, cleaner, mechanic, friend, community member, volunteer, etc. While to some it may seem impressive, the probability of depletion and burnout are real when we choose to sail our ship all alone.

Community Is All Around You

When we realize that each of our individual choices impacts a greater whole, you can see the entire expanse of community. One of my favorite examples of this interconnectedness is aspen trees. Have you ever noticed that you never see just one aspen? The reason is that each tree is actually a small part of a larger organism. The entire stand or group of trees is considered a single organism connected underground by its extensive root system that supports the entire community.

Being connected within the tapestry of life means that we are connected to the entire world and every living thing. One of the ways we are connected is by an unseen system, our breath. Our exchange of oxygen for carbon dioxide with the trees demonstrates the community we have formed through our breath. In a similar way we have a relationship with the oceans, our ecosystems, the rain forests, the birds in the sky, and so many of the intelligent and intricate processes of the world around us.

This is why our community is more than just the people in our life. We can each have a relationship with nature, the animals, the sky, the ocean. For me, the moments I feel the most connected are when I have a sense of belonging to something bigger. This usually occurs when I'm in nature. Dusk is my favorite time to commune with the natural world. That's when I actually feel like life is more than just the minutiae of every day. Instead, it's a palpable, living tapestry that reminds me how much I belong.

ONE DEGREE SHIFT INQUIRY:
How Are You Connected?

Grab a blanket. Lay it out on the floor. Pull on the lower right-hand corner of the blanket. What happened? Did you see that tugging on one part impacted the whole blanket?

Now, how does this relate to you and your relationship with community? If we are each an individual thread in the blanket, where can you see that you are already impacting someone or something else?

We are always in this experience of life together. We can be awakened and begin to recognize this intercon- nectedness, or we can stay unconscious to how our be- haviors may cause harm and continue to hurt others.

The lesson of community is learning how to skillfully contribute—whether it be to our family, our work, to those we socialize with, or to organizations we believe in. The challenge of community is that together we can either create something beautiful or something harmful. If you are singing in a choir, do you want to create beautiful music, or do you want to create a cacophony?

Be Open to Diversity in Community

A community can be a relationship between two or more people: it doesn't need to be a lot of people. We can begin to create community in our day-to-day life by starting where we are. Communities can have the common purpose of a goal and a way of relating to others. If this is what you are looking for, start a group, such as a parent group, a poetry group, a meditation group. Whatever interests you, there is a way to create a space to bring people together to explore, learn, and nourish deeper connections.

The power of a community doesn't have to occur when every- one agrees or holds the same values all the time. Life can become stagnant when we aren't exposed to other viewpoints, passions, or opportunities to learn something new. In fact, our world is complex, and there is plenty of room for us to be welcoming of differences.

This aspect of community is so important right now when our world can, at times, seem so divisive. When we begin to see the world as one family, we can start to shift our behaviors. And one of the gifts within this family is the access to differing perspectives, backgrounds, and experiences. We need to hear and see these differences because we will never be able to hold the entire picture of what is going on around us. In many ways we have inherited our perspective from our ancestors' successes and sorrows, which were based on the choices they made. The choices we are making today will influence future generations and will also become the past that our children and grandchildren will inherit and have to navigate. Because this is true, no one person can ever see the whole story; we cannot know everything that came before every one of us, or how we each see the world right now. This is why we need each other: to break through our singular viewpoint and gain insights into what others believe about the same experience.

There are plenty of people who are not the same as you, whether you define yourself by race, sexual preference or identity, or political viewpoints. This diversity is actually a gift because it can inspire us to pause and reflect on our choices while at the same time hold on to the ideas we're passionate about. If we can hold on to this notion we can learn to be in better relationships with people who have different views.

I know that this idea can be challenging, and for some, it is a big ask to take this leap. We can become entrenched, stuck in the mind frame that our ideas are right, and we can unconsciously act as if we are the center of the universe. And when we recognize that everybody is living their lives from a different worldview and that they may have something of value to share, we are invited to be open and stop being defensive, by putting our weapons down, taking our armor off, and getting curious about this alternative way of seeing.

The truth is, we can't change other people, especially those with whom we don't see eye to eye. What we can do is take responsibility for how we each show up—every moment of every day. Just by making this small shift from trying to convince others to change to working on how you engage can impact how we interact with others, and in return how they might respond differently to you. For instance, if I'm in a conversation with someone I don't agree with and I'm always showing up as the same old Coby with my same perspective, most likely the other person will continue to show up with their armor on and we both stay stuck in the status quo, rather than opening to the infinite possibilities of what we could create together.

One of my best childhood friends grew up with parents who were divorced. Even though they couldn't live together, and were no longer in love, they were willing to adopt a behavior that was cooperative for the sake of the impact it would have on their child. They made an agreement that they would always speak positively about each other in front of their child, and they would engage as a family for holidays and vacations. They would each shift their behavior enough so that the other person felt comfortable and able to relax and be at ease, so any potential triggers would be minimized when they were together. As a result, my friend grew up feeling that he was part of an amazing family. His community was able to survive even though there were real irreconcilable differences.

Is It Better to Give Than Receive?

Community reminds us that life is a two-way relationship between giving and receiving. Many people find it much easier to give, give, give. Yet when you receive you are actually letting another person feel better about themselves as they get to make an offering from their heart. What shifts when you are able to receive help, feedback, or compliments, and let your guard down?

Lean into Your Community

Yoga can provide potential solutions, yet it does not have an answer to every problem. Your community can include other teachers and people who can provide a different perspective or different tools to support you in the moments when you need help. In essence, a community can be a toolbox of resources.

Many years ago, I took a workshop where everyone was blindfolded and taken to a large maze out in a forest. The goal of the exercise was to find our way out as quickly as possible. Each time a person made it out, one of the facilitators would announce their escape to everybody else: "Nathan is out of the maze," "Susan is out of the maze."

I was pretty competitive at that time in my life, so I immediately decided that I was going to be the first one out of that maze. We put our blindfolds on, entered the maze, and—within less than a minute—I heard the announcement, "Aubrey is out of the maze." Wait, what? How had she gotten out so fast? I took a breath and refocused. Time went on, and I didn't seem any closer to finding my way out. One by one, I heard, "Mark is out of the maze. Todd is out of the maze. Jillian is out of the maze." I couldn't figure out why I wasn't getting out of this maze, and why everybody else had gotten out so easily. As each person got out of the maze I found myself more and more frustrated. I could hear people talking, yet I was more interested in getting myself out than listening to what they were saying. The facilitators came over to me and asked a number of times, "Coby, how are you doing?" My response was always, "I'm fine, please leave me alone, I'm trying to get out of the maze."

Twenty minutes went by; thirty minutes, an hour. By this time, everybody in the group was cheering me on because it was clear that I was the only person left in the maze. Finally, one of the facilitators came up to me and asked again, "Coby, how's it going?" I turned to him and said, "I don't know. I guess I need help." And the next words I heard were, "Coby is out of the maze."

It turned out that the maze was not a maze at all—it was a totally enclosed course with no exit, unless you asked for help. In that moment, I realized how often I'd been stuck in the maze of life, stuck in a riptide, and forgetting that the wide-open door was right there, if I only reached out and asked someone for help.

Is going at it alone always the best use of your energy? My guess is, probably not. You don't need to do it all. Just because you can do everything doesn't mean you need to do everything. See what happens when you let yourself lean into community, lean into family, lean into your tribe.

You are never alone in the maze. While you are building your community, look for the people you know you could ask for help. In reality, there are many resources present in every community that could offer support, like therapists, community centers, food banks, or simply opening yourself up to a person sitting next to you.

ONE DEGREE SHIFT INQUIRY:
Are You in the Maze?

- Where are you stuck in the maze?
- What could potentially shift if you asked for support?
- What would it be like to ask for help?

- Who could you ask for help?
- When is a time you supported someone else to get out of the maze? What was the impact and value of supporting someone else?

Community Invites Participation

Everyone in our community is riding their waves too, and may not be able to show up for us the way we want when we ask them for help. They may be dealing with their gremlins or riding a wave of grief, sadness, or sorrow. They may want to help you, but don't know how in the moment you are asking. Or, they may actually not have the capacity to show up. That doesn't mean you are not worthy of someone else's support.

You may need to find someone else in your community you can turn to this time. There is also value in seeking out professional help such as a therapist, counselor, or support group. There's never any harm in having as many perspectives available that can help and support you. And just like any relationship, not every therapist or support group will automatically be the right fit. When seeking out professional help, make sure you feel like it's a good match for you.

Just like there will be moments when you will need to ask for help, to be a contributing member of a community means that you will also be called upon to help others. Showing up for others is a small shift that can deepen your connections within the community. And being there for others is a building block for creating trust: when we are there for one another in moments of need as well as celebration, we can experience the feeling of fully belonging, and that we matter. An aspect of yoga is being of service, and the gift is knowing that you can support others.

Create Community

To create community, you're invited to put yourself out there.

- Put yourself in new social experiments. You might need to stretch yourself in places that don't seem to fit your authentic self for the sake of expanding and simply enjoying the company of those you wouldn't typically interact with. By doing this, your worldview begins to expand, and the world becomes a more intimate and accessible place. Consider dance classes, art classes, yoga classes at a different studio; join a master's swim team; or volunteer.

- Commit to talking to three strangers a day. You never know who you will meet—you might find a new best friend.

- Have a meal with someone at work you don't typically eat with, and allow the conversation to begin with curiosity about them.

- Leave your phone at home to create space for more connections. You'll be amazed at how much more capacity you have to pay attention to the world around you. That's where you'll see those opportunities to talk to people, help others, and recognize your impact.

- Take time to share what you value in others. Tell people what you see in them—the good stuff—and make sure you are being sincere! When people feel seen, they are usually more open to connection.

Your Sacred Community, Your *Kula*

In yoga, one quality of consciousness is the *kula*, which can be thought of as the "community of the heart." The kula is an integral subsection of your community, an essential resource on the path to becoming more authentically yourself. The people in your sacred community can talk to you with radical honesty, are willing to stick by you through the most challenging times, and are there to celebrate you in your greatest victories. They are people you can practice cleaning up your messes with; they are people you can try on your authentic self with; and they will be willing to shine a light on your blind spots and the moments when you are in the shadow of your energetic impact. Your sacred community is willing to listen on a deeper plane than surface conversation. They are also there to enjoy the simple pleasures, to laugh, and to create sweet memories.

Friends are the people in your community with whom you socialize because you enjoy their company. Your sacred community is a deeper life bond. You may have heard the expression "a reason, a season, or a lifetime." Often people who are simply friends come in for a reason or a season, while people in your sacred community will be there for you for a lifetime.

And as we participate in a sacred community, we have the ability to individually become more authentic. We can see that the choices we make affect others, because we're a thread within the tapestry. We can honor one another's unique gifts instead of focusing on our faults. We can help others recognize their blind spots and gremlins, and see our own in the process. We can call one another forth, highlighting the potential in someone else and holding that space and helping them to grow into it.

There's also great value in making space for lightness and

laughter with your kula: there is meaning even when the conversations and time together don't appear to have deep purpose. If you're interested in creating a healthy community, a healthy world, what if part of the solution was to play, have adventures, and relax together? What if we as a community could take a step back and just cherish and savor the small moments of connectedness?

During my early years of studying yoga, I was introduced to this idea of a sacred community, and though I had a large group of friends, I was interested in finding my kula and making deeper connections. When I reflected on who was already in my life, I felt blessed that my mom, dad, family, and a few childhood friends were part of my kula. Yet I still longed for more. Although I continued to meet many wonderful people, it took time until I found Danny Arguetty and Katie Brauer. My relationships with these two people have become opportunities to support one another in evolving into the greatest versions of ourselves. The three of us champion one another along in our individual and linked journeys. We also challenge one another and shine light on potential blind spots, all from a place of love and care.

ONE DEGREE SHIFT INQUIRY:
Who Is in Your Sacred Community?

Your kula can be there to support you in moments of success and in moments when you are feeling out of alignment.

Draw a large circle and place a dot in the center. This dot represents you. Inside the circle, use different colored markers or pens, and place dots that represent those who are part of your sacred community. Label the dots in accordance to who you feel closest to, from the center outward. Outside of the ring, place dots for the people who are in your regular community: your friends and family who may not be a part of your sacred community.

- Did you expect that your friends and sacred community would overlap?
- What are some qualities you appreciate in your sacred community?
- What are some qualities you appreciate about your friends?
- How do those in your sacred community support you?
- How do those in your sacred community call you forth?
- How do you support those in your sacred community? What is one small thing you could do today to show your appreciation for them?
- What keeps you caring for each other?
- What else would you include in your sacred community? Animals, plants, or other aspects of nature? How do these make you feel connected?
- Do you believe in a higher power, a force that carries insight and guidance? If so, how is it a part of your sacred community? What impact does it have on you?

Finding Sacred Community

It can be a challenge to begin cultivating a true sacred community— we can get stuck in our routines, or we may have lost the courage to put ourselves out there and meet new people. And for some, as you dive more into your authentic self, you may find you are outgrowing people you once thought of as friends and realize you are longing for different and new connections.

The first step to finding your kula could be putting yourself in the same experiment as you did finding your community. Then, there is a conscious creation for these deeper connections where you can be your most authentic self, with whom you can be the most vulnerable, raw, and real. Having more intimate conversations, showing up for the people you really care about, making sacrifices for them, and getting curious about their needs will help you create a deeper relationship with the members of the community you decide are worth investing your time, emotional resources, and attention into.

One way to find your kula is practicing using powerful dynamic questions and inquiring with people. We all want to be seen, loved, and heard, and when people feel understood they are more likely to feel a sense of trust and safety, and ultimately will be more open to having a deeper relationship. The overall quality of dynamic inquiring is sincere curiosity on your part: asking for a thoughtful response rather than looking for a yes/no answer. They are open-ended questions that create conversation. The questions will lead to answers that can create opportunities for greater clarity, possibility, or new learning.

By engaging in dynamic questions, inquiring, and sincerely being curious about another person, you can enhance a new or existing relationship. Rather than asking someone the standard "How are you?" consider some of the following conversation inquiries. My favorite prompts such as "Tell me more," "Say more," and "What else?" allow for deeper and juicier answers:

- Tell me about something you long for. Describe what it looks like. What's one small step you can take right now to get you there?
- What has passion and meaning for you?
- What does fulfillment mean to you?
- What were you born to do? What is important about this?
- When have you felt most alive? What were you doing? Who were you with?
- If you had a magic wand what would you do? What excites you about that? What is important about that?

Conscious Communication: Skillfully Engage with Your Community

Whether you are focusing on your new community or your sacred community, just like a garden, we need to tend to it—we need to take care of it for it to survive and to grow. We're invited to be present and to stay curious. By giving your time and attention, you are offering one of the most precious gifts you can give.

Part of the responsibility of tending to your community is showing up as the best version of yourself and inspiring others to do the same. Conscious communication is about being present, open, and fully engaging in a conversation. Your relationships in community will deepen when you make a safe space for other people to share their thoughts and feelings without you having the need to jump in and fix, problem solve, or interpret what they are saying. This skill involves various forms of active listening, creating an internal boundary with yourself to stay present, to not respond, and to hold loving space. Yoga teaches this as *asrutkarna*, the art of listening attentively.

Co-listening is a form of conscious communication that allows people to feel more heard, while those listening gain a better understanding of the speaker and learn something about their own habits and internal judgments. It is the practice where one person listens to another without interpreting, problem solving, analyzing, helping, or discussing the content of what is being conveyed. The listener is listening from the witness consciousness, simply being present with their full attention on the speaker. The listener is like a mountain: in this role we don't ask questions, nod, or show other nonverbal conversation cues; or touch, hug, or physically console. We are simply present to compassionately listen.

Sometimes there are hard conversations to be had, and one aspect of being in a community is to be open to the process of engagement, without shutting people down and making them feel defensive. These interactions can be exhausting when each person feels like they are defending a position. What's really happening is that we stop listening and being open to both sides. If somebody is in a defensive mode and stuck on defending their point, and at the same time you are defending yours, it creates a dead end to the conversation. If we are willing to hold the relationship as a priority over the need to be right, the place to start is to remain curious and actually listen. While listening openly might not change either person's position, at least it invites in presence and ability for each individual to feel fully heard, which just by itself can soften preexisting armor.

Another conscious communication tool related to asrutkarna is reflective listening. Often people don't feel heard or understood in the process of conversation, particularly because so many people are distracted when speaking to others (from their own internal dialogue or by technology). Too often people are just waiting to respond, or waiting to speak, and never really listen. Reflective listening resolves this as it is simply the process of mirroring back to the person speaking what you heard them say. It doesn't have to be verbatim; it could be a general summary of what was spoken.

For example, if someone is sharing about a hard time they are having with an aging parent, you would simply respond in a way that feels natural for you, something like, "It sounds like navigating the situation with your parents is challenging," and then ask, "Did I hear you right?" For many people, having this reflection provides a sense of calm and deeper connection, a small shift that's extremely potent.

Reflective listening is a technique that is used in many different fields, from therapy to yoga teacher training, and is meant to provide a way for us to ensure that we are being as present as we can be when someone is speaking. It allows you to see if you are hearing the other person fully, or if you are hearing what they say through your own life filters or preconceived internal judgments.

Reflective listening is also useful with kids (and adults), especially when you want both to honor where they are at and hold a certain boundary. For example, if your teenager is upset that you won't let them stay out late and go to an unsupervised party, you might say, "I get that you are frustrated with our decision and we still feel that this is the right choice right now. Is there anything more you want to say? Is there anything we didn't hear right? Is there any information we are missing?"

What I Like About You

One of my favorite games to play is, "One thing I like (or love) about you is…" I love taking the time to share very specific things I appreciate about the people in my community. Learning to verbalize what is great about others can shift your perspective about those around you, and possibly yourself as well.

Ask five people what are three things they love about you. Ask them to be as specific as possible. Notice how you feel receiving this gift of positive affirmation: Can you allow yourself to be seen this way without deflecting, feeling embarrassed, or self-deprecating?

Then, tell five people in your community or sacred community what things you love about them. Be as specific as you can.

How did this inquiry make you feel?

Practicing the *Yamas*

Another way to support a community is by taking a contemporary perspective of the yogic teachings called the *yamas*: the five principles that support building character, which can lead to healthier engagement with others. The word "yama" often gets translated as "constraints." I believe a more welcoming definition is when it gets translated as a "bridle," the headgear used to steer a horse. We can think of the yamas as suggestions for living that can steer us in a life-affirming direction. And just like the reigns on a horse, most of the time you don't need to hold on too tightly; a loose grip can produce a more desirable result as you work with the intelligence of the horse or, in this case, life.

The yamas are guidelines for how we can engage with life in a positive way. By practicing the yamas, you are more likely to act in accordance with your highest self. By doing so, you are more likely to engage with your community from a more grounded, clear, and loving place—which can lead to a more supportive and productive community. Like with so many yogic teachings, while these five principles are described separately, they dovetail, inform, and work with one another to support us as we navigate our path.

For the next five days, focus each day on one of the yamas, and journal about your experience. How did focusing on this yama impact your own sense of fulfillment and well-being? How did it impact your relationships? How did you feel?

Ahimsa

The first yama is *ahimsa*, which we've learned means to cause no harm. Like accountability, it encompasses kindness, compassion, and understanding. To me, the deeper meaning of ahimsa is that we need to be responsible for our choices.

Ahimsa could truly be a lifelong practice. If we always paused to reflect and asked ourselves before we did anything if what we were about to do would cause harm to ourselves or another, I believe we would live in a very different world. Some people choose to practice ahimsa by eating less meat, or being conscious about their purchases (e.g., fair trade), while others employ kindness in their relationships with neighbors or work colleagues (especially when they feel triggered or irritated). Ahimsa is also a practice that invites us to work with ourselves, to put attention on our thoughts, to soothe our gremlins, and to do the best we can.

Now, like everything, there are varying degrees of this idea as it lives on a spectrum. There are communities around the world that believe stepping on an insect is harmful. While you may or may not disagree with this perspective, what if you could be that sensitive to the world around you? Can you see the ways you are being unkind to yourself or others? What areas of your life need to shift to cultivate a more nurturing and gentle way of being?

ONE DEGREE SHIFT INQUIRY:
Ahimsa Affirmation

I am kind, I am compassionate, and I value myself and others. My thoughts and actions are focused on loving awareness. I nurture and cherish others and myself. I am aware that the mind sometimes entertains thoughts of fear, anger, or selfishness. I hold space for these thoughts as well as clear boundaries to minimize their power.

Satya

Satya means truth, and it encompasses being honest, genuine, authentic; owning feelings, practicing conscious communication, and having integrity. It's about discovering your own truth, speaking your truth, and then living it. Part of the yoga path is to unpack your truth by stripping away what does not feel true for you. As you grow and evolve, and incorporate other people's perspectives into your own, you will come to recognize with humility what is real and true for you.

Satya teaches us that we can live in a community where there are multiple viewpoints of truth. A way to practice satya in a community is to be courageous enough to speak your truth while honoring *ahimsa*. For instance, when someone tells you their truth, can you step back and hold that their truth is valuable for them, even if you disagree? Can you agree to disagree? Or, when you are speaking, can you pause and ask yourself: Is that true? Is that really true? If it doesn't feel 100 percent accurate, clarify what you mean. And, if you make a mistake or feel like you are at fault, apologize right away; set the record straight and keep the integrity of truth.

> ## ONE DEGREE SHIFT INQUIRY:
> ### Satya Affirmation
>
> I honor my truth. I speak the truth to myself and to others while practicing *ahimsa*. When offering my truth in the form of feedback, I am sensitive to the feelings of others. I speak the truth in the spirit of love and wrap my words with kindness and empathy.

Asteya

Asteya invites us to notice where we are devaluing or stealing from both ourselves and others. It can be applied to physical things, time, or attention. It means providing for oneself without taking what is not yours. It invites you to focus on taking responsibility for providing for yourself in the world, and recognizing the abundance of life and the infinite resources that are always available to you. It can mean not stealing time by always dominating a conversation, or checking in with someone before you start talking to see if they have the time to connect.

In community, asteya teaches that we can honor someone's talents and contributions without feeling less than. You can acknowledge others' successes with gratitude and without envy. You recognize that there are enough resources, possibilities, and love for everyone.

ONE DEGREE SHIFT INQUIRY:
Asteya Affirmation

I live in gratitude for all I have. I take and use only what is rightfully mine. I am conscious of my use of natural resources. I respect the possessions, time, and talents of others.

Aparigraha

Aparigraha invites us to notice when we have become possessive or attached in a way that depletes us. It is letting go of belongings, ideas, and people that no longer enhance our fulfillment and vitality. It allows you to honor that which is of high value to you, and every once in a while, to give something you love away. For example, you may still have your childhood toys, and you feel connected to them for nostalgic reasons. But by donating them to children in need, you are practicing aparigraha.

When you take only what is needed, you are also leaving more for others. And your willingness to practice aparigraha and to give something up, even something you love, creates a gift for someone else in your community.

ONE DEGREE SHIFT INQUIRY:
Aparigraha Affirmation

I release my attachment to other people, substances, and ideas that deplete my vitality. I honor myself as I cultivate a lifestyle of simplicity and generosity. I recognize the difference between a "want" and a "need."

Brahmacharya

Brahmacharya traditionally refers to practicing celibacy. A more modern interpretation is our ability to learn how to harness energy or recognize how we are using it. There is a saying, "Where attention goes energy flows." Your energy can be affected by lifestyle choices such as food, physical activity, relationships, or even your internal thoughts. When you become sensitive to where you place your attention and the choices you make, you can create a more desirable outcome based on the situation you are navigating. For instance, while it is totally natural to have challenging periods in friendships, with family, or in intimate relationships, if you were to step back and take an average, would you see a pattern of being depleted or uplifted? Many people get stuck in the fog and don't realize how depleted they have become. Are there other areas of your life that are draining you? What shift can you make to gain more vitality?

When you practice brahmacharya, you can see how you can devote your energy, and how it can positively impact your community. You can use this reclaimed energy to support your community's needs and become an active contributor.

ONE DEGREE SHIFT INQUIRY:
Brahmacharya Affirmation

I have great respect for my energy, and use it in ways that create optimal balance. When I feel off or disconnected, I trust my ability to look at my life and see what needs to shift and have the strength to do so.

Thank you for being my chosen family,
my tribe,
my most sacred community.
With you by my side
I feel at home in myself.
Empowered to be
exactly who I am,
and who I will become.

Instinctive Meditation

. . . I'm not a collection of incantations
Known only to experts.
I'm not a ladder to be climbed,
A sequence for piercing energy centers in your body.
I'm not to be found at the end of a long road.
I am right here.
. . .
I am beyond measure. I cannot be calculated.
I am beyond space and time.
I'm beyond ancient, and beyond the future.
There are no directions to me.
I am always here.
I am the embrace of your most intimate experience.

Though I am beyond the intellect,
I am not beyond your daring.

I am the nourishing state of fullness
That is the essence of soul.
You belong to me, and I am yours.

. . .

Sacred texts sing of my reality,
But I cannot be found in them,
For I am the one listening.
I am always closer than the breath.

. . .

I am everywhere, infusing everything.
To find me,
Become absorbed in intense experience.
Go all the way.
Be drenched in the energies of life.
Enter the world beyond separation.

The light of a candle reveals a room.
The rays of the sun reveal the world.
So does the divine feminine
Illumine the way to me.

—*from* The Radiance Sutras

Meditation seems to be the answer to everything these days; an antidote to busy lives, a way to de-stress and be present, a technique for managing anxiety, a tool to increase focus and productivity, a way to tap back into simplicity, and a conduit to a greater sense of fulfillment. And meditation seems to be for everyone, from yoga practitioners to politicians, corporate executives, professional athletes, school administrators, and students at all levels of the education system. Meditation is in vogue. It's the buzz-word of the yoga world and beyond right now. Many people I know feel like they *should* be meditating because it's the "in" thing.

I had been meditating for decades before I began training aspiring meditation teachers and meditation coaches with my teacher, Dr. Lorin Roche. One of my deepest passions is to share his approach to meditation, as I see it as one of the most beautiful and life-affirming gifts one could receive. It is liberating, refreshing, and full of healing, joy, and tenderness. It is a practice for those of us longing to connect at the deepest level with ourselves and others.

And though I believe most everyone would benefit from meditating, I wouldn't say that meditation is the answer for *everything*; it is a useful tool to have in your toolbox so you can better ride the waves of life. Think of it as another experiment or inquiry that can help you learn more about yourself.

We do know that meditation can help the body and mind recharge, refresh, and reconnect. It can provide the mental space to become more aware of our deepest desires. It can help us engage our inner compass so we can make decisions that bring us closer to more fulfillment and well-being, and point to where we feel stuck. The practice can strengthen our ability to be with the moment, pause before taking an action, and step back to simply look at what is showing up in any situation.

Meditation is an integral part of yoga. It is also an opportunity to be in awe and delight with the miracle of life and to cherish and nourish your life force, or *prana*. It is an intimate relationship with yourself, and can help you see more of what your life has to offer, so that you can appreciate the beauty and intimacy that is always available.

For me, meditation provides an opportunity to fall in love with life, or as Lorin says, "to embrace the primordial cosmic energy—the seed from which all of life blossoms"—referred to in yoga as *pranashakti*. Everything we experience is pranashakti expressing itself, whether it is a flower blooming, the ache we feel when we remember we stopped living fully, the cycles of the moon, or laughing with friends. When you meditate and tap into this energy, you might notice a softening in your defensive armor and an ability to better engage in the ultimate trusting of the human experience, the highs and lows, the twists and turns, the knowing and the not knowing. You can feel more at home in yourself and the world around you; you are more able to trust and better navigate the rhythms of life.

Yet many people avoid stepping into this potent practice. They may believe they won't be able to "quiet their mind" or sit still long enough to feel the impact. They worry that they can't commit the time or that they aren't doing it right. Or they fear what might come up if they take time to dive into and explore their inner world.

So let me put you at ease. The crash course on meditation in this chapter is radically different than anything you may have heard or read about before. This approach is *not* about quieting your mind or the body, and it doesn't require that you sit still for even one minute if you don't want to. The truth is, meditation is a natural human behavior that you have already experienced. You just didn't know you were doing it.

Think of the moments when you felt drawn toward something, whether it was looking into a child's eyes, skiing down a perfectly groomed mountain, losing yourself in a novel, or looking out the window during a lightning storm. Any or all of these kinds of moments pulled you into an experience and held you there, even if the moment was fleeting. You were able to become absorbed in that one moment and melt into it: you became fully infused with the experience, saturated by your senses. And then in a flash, you may have awakened to other thoughts, feelings, or emotions.

So was that meditation? Absolutely. And so was the moment when you began to wonder what was for dinner, or felt a twinge of sadness toward a loss. The entire journey from complete saturation into any other activity of the mind is meditation. All of it. And within the two parts to the journey, neither was better nor more important than the other.

Lorin teaches that this type of meditation is an internal journey known as a *yatra*. Think of it like an adventure into your inner world. And just like there are usually parts of an adventure or trip that are easeful and magical, there are often times where there can be a struggle or challenge. Meditation is both the easeful and restful moments *and* the moments of restlessness.

This practice is called instinctive meditation. It can provide a time to rejuvenate, or an opportunity to hone into desires so deep you might not be carving out time to even recognize them in your normal, everyday experiences. In this approach, we are trying to align with the intelligence of nature and life itself, not transcend it.

Instinctive meditation may feel different from what you have heard about meditation or what you are already practicing, especially if you have been meditating for years. Think of this chapter as an invitation to be open to a new perspective. You might *love* your current meditation practice, and if you do, I want you to cherish it. However, see if you can put it aside, and after reading the chapter and trying out the meditations, you can decide which practice you want to keep. Maybe both, maybe neither. The willingness to put down your current practice for the sake of learning something new might just be the one degree shift that could change the course of your life.

Meet Lorin Roche

Everything I know about instinctive meditation comes from Dr. Lorin Roche. His approach to meditation is a practice that calls you to the heart. When I first met him, I let go of everything I thought meditation was, and he introduced me to a world beyond words—some of the most profound and intimate experiences I have had.

I think of Lorin as a mad scientist of the heart, a magician of the soul. He is the most joyful person I have ever met, and lives in a state of wonder and awe. He has the curiosity of a child, the presence of a wise elder, and the sense of an accomplished master—though he would never describe himself this way.

Among his many achievements has been his poetic interpretation of an ancient yoga text called the *Vijnana Bhairava Tantra*, which he refers to as *The Radiance Sutras*. Reading this book is like listening to a conversation between two lovers, where one is longing to experience more of the divine in everyday life and the other offers the 112 doorways into meditation, almost like an instruction manual. Each of the 112 sutras shows how we can access the divine right now.

The Radiance Sutras is an instruction book on meditation, and it's the most beautiful thing I've ever read. Not only has it shaped the way I look at meditation, it's also shaped the way I look at life. For instance, when I read sutra twenty-six there was a knocking at my heart, a call that I simply could not ignore.

> *The One Who is at play everywhere said,*
> *There is a place in the heart where everything meets.*
> *Go there if you want to find me.*
> *Mind, senses, soul, eternity, all are there.*
> *Are you there?*
> *Enter the bowl of vastness that is the heart.*
> *Give yourself to it with total abandon.*

Quiet ecstasy is there
And a steady, regal sense of resting in a perfect spot.
Once you know the way
The nature of attention will call you
To return, again and again,
And be saturated with knowing,
"I belong here, I am at home here."
Answer that call.

Reading this sutra invited me into a profound one degree shift. It awakened something inside of me that I couldn't deny. It encouraged me to take the first steps on what would become an incredible journey—both beautiful and painful, where I experienced the deepest love and deepest heartbreak, and through this practice of meditation, I learned to cherish it all—that it was all beautiful.

Lorin teaches that the divine is all around us in every moment, and that we don't need to take drugs, drink, go on a vision quest, or travel to India to feel alive or to access the beautiful and sweet moments of our day-to-day. His approach invites you to pay loving attention to the rhythms of life, and when you do, you will feel more connected to life itself and have greater access to vitality and aliveness.

Principles for Instinctive Meditation

There are many differences between the classical forms of meditation you may have tried and this approach. The first is the fact that whatever you may have heard about meditation or the instructions you have been given were not necessarily intended for "householders," the everyday people like us. In fact, there are many different types of meditation practices, and they exist on a spectrum from more traditional to more progressive. The meditation practices at the very end of the traditional side were specifically created thousands of years ago for renunciative monks, a distinct group of men whose goal was to transcend the human experience, and who could devote their whole life to this one journey by sequestering themselves away from the world. The aim of this type of monk was to merge with the divine and to know his true nature: to discover who he was before he was born, and who he'll be after he takes his final exhale. They believe that much of the struggles in the daily lives that householders like us experience were just unnecessary illusions, and so the human experience, including the random thoughts that pop into our heads, were not real and should be transcended or surpassed.

The practice for householders, on the other hand, is not about leaving the body or quieting the mind—though you may experience these things while you are meditating. Instead, it's about celebrating life, savoring it, seeing the sweetness in each moment, and welcoming all the moments and thoughts that come with the gift of being alive. Instinctive meditation is common sense meditation. This is a practice where we are bonding with our souls and our bodies, a practice created especially for people who live *in* the world and want to have a healthy relationship with their attachments and what they love. This is a practice that reveres individuality and the balance of attaching and letting go. This is a practice that delights in being alive, and in wonder and awe of everything all around.

The difference between these approaches to meditation is in the instructions you may have heard that go with more classical meditation—sit still, empty the mind of your thoughts, focus on your breath—which do not always support us householders, who are learning to navigate living *in* the world. We aren't trying to transcend anything, we want to live our earthly lives with more joy and ease.

The goal of quieting the mind makes more sense in the context of a monk's life. If we were monks who renounced the earthly world, we would be living in *ashrams* or communities where our basic needs like water, food, and shelter were taken care of. It also would mean that you never had to worry about romantic relationships, money, or meaning and purpose—which would allow our minds to become pretty calm. However, this idea of stilling the mind, or ceasing the fluctuations of the mind, does not take into account how the human brain actually functions. Our brain has a default mode that kicks into gear when we have a rare moment of silence or calm. That's when the brain can time travel, relive our past, or plan for the future. It can make us aware of various scenarios (i.e., worry) to make sure we are safe. So, as a householder who has responsibilities in the world, it's totally normal that when you meditate you think about family, work, purpose, or relationships. In this approach to meditation we celebrate the movement of thoughts and our to-do list as part of the beautiful tapestry of life!

So while there may be moments during meditation where you may have more space between your thoughts or pockets of quiet—that is not the ultimate goal! This supposed prerequisite of silencing the mind can actually create more of a mental drain as many people get caught up, stressed, and even anxious when their minds act naturally and thoughts continue to flow in and out. Instead, in this approach we're going to learn how to ride the waves of our thoughts and celebrate their fluctuations. As Lorin beautifully says, "We don't have minds that wander, we have minds that wonder."

It's true: we're curious creatures with fully functioning brains, so don't feel bad if you can't quiet your mind. This is a one degree shift, realizing that what you thought was a must-have condition for meditation (quieting the mind) was in fact not meant for you *at all*, so hopefully this might reset your expectations. You have permission to stop chastising yourself about your frustrations with meditation, your attention span, or judging yourself for "doing it wrong." Instead, practice *ahimsa*, be kind to yourself, and embrace the first rule of instinctive meditation. As Lorin teaches, "No internal spanking and no internal shaming." You are going to have thoughts; it's part of the process, it's beautiful, it's natural. This is why I suggest putting aside what you think you know about meditation.

For instance, I once went through an experience where I felt like I got hit by the cosmic two-by-four. Following a heartbreak filled with sorrow and grief at a level I had really never experienced before, I felt emotionally annihilated. During that time I was meditating, but it felt too challenging to be with the practice because I was overwhelmed with sadness and the ache in my heart, and my mind was all over the place. A few months later I went to see Lorin. I told him, "It's too hard to meditate, this pain is too much. What should I do?" He just looked at me and said, "It's just so beautiful, Coby. You're just experiencing sorrow and grief."

At the time I didn't quite get it. But looking back, I can now see that my meditation practice was healing me—even in my sadness and with all the other thoughts that were moving through me. It was a reminder that during meditation, we can work out the aches and the pains of the human experience. My meditation practice was not about just sticking to a specific technique; it was about welcoming the healing nature of meditation. My mind didn't wander away, but rather it led me to tending to my heart and to having a more intimate relationship with life itself. This time in my life was a beautiful reminder of the gift of walking a path of yoga and meditation as a householder, walking this path where sometimes we're going to love so deeply that we're also going to grieve so deeply. I realized that my emotions were a beautiful and difficult part of being human, and not something that I needed to cut myself off from. My meditation allowed me to hold them, cherish them, and tend to them.

So instead of beating yourself up when your mind supposedly wanders, welcome whatever arises, because it is the nature of *pranashakti*, the primordial cosmic energy. It has a pulsation, or *spanda*, the sacred tremor of life. Spanda shows us there is always movement, which includes both moments of rest and activity, like an inhale and an exhale and the pause in between the two. Part of a living yoga and meditation practice is to connect and explore this pulse.

The truth is rest, restlessness, and anticipation are part of human nature. Once we recognize that life is this dance between rest and restlessness, we no longer have to judge ourselves for having a brain that works or a body that wants to move, heal, rest, and recharge.

It's also natural for people in the pull and excitement of life's force to find themselves looking for more than what is in front of them. It is pulsating through you all day, every day. Since the life force is always moving, nothing in life is ever completely still, so why should your actions go against nature? Instinctive meditation can happen anywhere at any time, whether you are on your meditation cushion or going for a walk.

The second principle for instinctive meditation is cultivating the ability to welcome all parts of yourself to the experience, including the ones that you may not always feel friendly toward. We are all a complete range of personas, from the kind, generous, and loving to the judgmental, competitive, and stubborn. In this approach we welcome the fullness of the human experience, which includes emotions, thoughts, memories, fantasies, etc., and don't see them as problems to be solved. At the same time, these aspects may be connected to thoughts or ideas that are wanting to be sorted out. As Lorin says, "The ache in your heart is holy." Meditation can be a time when we allow the intelligence of the life force to heal us. The primary attitude is to welcome every emotion or thought as it arises and fades away.

The third principle is that pranashakti offers immense wisdom and support during meditation. Your *prana*, or life force, wants you to heal, recharge, relax, repair, and renew. It wants you to come home to who you really are. It wants you to find your center. Meditation can bring up the old aches and pains of our past, and remind us of experiences that were long forgotten or never properly processed. For example, you may have never fully integrated the grief of a loss, or the anguish of an illness. When these memories reveal themselves, it can feel intense, and it is your choice whether to follow and tend to these feelings or return to the meditation practice you began with. If you choose to stay with what is arising, even if it is uncomfortable, you are giving yourself an opportunity to let the wisdom and support of pranashakti move through you, like a massage for your heart, soul, or spirit.

Imagine that you have a friend who is pregnant with triplets. She's on her way to the hospital and her partner says to her, "I don't love you. I never loved you, and I'll bet you those children aren't even mine. I'm leaving you right now." At the same time she gets a phone call that her mother, whom she was very close to, has just died. There is no time to process all of this: she goes into labor and gives birth to the triplets. Then life goes into overdrive: she needs to take care of her babies.

Let's say five years go by, and this friend starts meditating. All of a sudden she starts to cry. She feels the heartbreak, or the ache of her own heart, the sorrow, the pain, or the grief she didn't have time to process when she had to go into primal mode. This is when life force is massaging her spirit and saying, "We're going to work this out." Because life force is self-correcting, and wants us to be in a state of health, vitality, and radiance. All of this can happen during meditation.

The fourth principle is that instinctive meditation does not have a particular time commitment. You can meditate anytime and any-where, though it can be beneficial to have a set time in the day that you like to do it (although don't try meditating while you're driving). I like meditating in the beginning of my day. It can last as long as you want, or be as short as one minute. And by all means, it's okay to fall asleep in meditation: most people are so exhausted and would benefit if their meditation practice was to nap every day for the next year. Yes, that really could be your meditation. Trust the intelligence of your body. If your body asks for rest, give it permission to recharge, allow it to heal.

A New Language for Meditation

Instinctive meditation asks you to explore what interests you, what you find soothing or delightful. Rather than imposing a technique filled with "shoulds" or feeling like you are going through some sort of dog training for the mind, as in "sit" and "stay"—the new language invites you into the inquiries that allow you to savor, infuse, immerse, engage, orient, imagine, connect to, allow, and explore.

Language holds power, and shifting just a few words can greatly influence someone's experience of meditation. These small shifts in language are one degree revolutions in themselves! For instance, if you've ever attended a meditation class, you may have been told that your scattered thinking is a "monkey mind," and that meditation will teach you how to tame it. That is why you will hear the instructions, "If your mind wanders, bring it back," so often. To me, this monkey-mind language can be a bit misleading: Why would you shame your beautiful brain that is functioning exactly the way it is supposed to be working into thinking it's doing something wrong? You have a mind that's alive and curious, and this is a beautiful part of being human. And remember, minds don't wander, they wonder!

Here's another example: Instead of "Concentrate on your breathing," what shifts when you hear, "Take a few moments to explore what interests you in the rhythm and flow of your breathing." Breath is the relationship between what is inside of you and the outside world. Instinctive meditation welcomes us to explore this relationship from a place of desire and genuine interest, as opposed to the mandate to "concentrate."

Old Language	New Language
Concentrate on your breathing.	Explore what interests you in the rhythm and flow of your breathing.
Withdraw from your senses.	Delight in your senses.
Focus.	Hold, cherish, melt into.
Notice.	Welcome, feel, sense.
Bring your attention back.	What is more interesting right now? What is asking for your attention most right now?

Six Steps to Instinctive Meditation

Here are some suggestions on how you can begin to practice instinctive meditation. And even these instructions have choices you can make to tailor the experience to your needs. Before you begin, you may want to journal or write down your to-do list: What do you want to put aside so you can enjoy your practice? Or not! You may want to meditate on what's ahead of you just for the day. Some people like to exercise before they meditate so they can feel more comfortable in their body. I enjoy doing some kind of movement or breath work before my practice. You can do whatever resonates with you most!

Step 1: Choose a time of day and a location to practice. Place yourself into any posture that is comfortable. Let go of the idea that you need to sit cross-legged. Trust the intelligence of your own body, that it knows what it needs. If you want to sit in a chair, lie down, stand up, move or sway during your practice, that is perfect! A meditation can happen when you're in the shower, just letting yourself feel the water run down on you. If it feels natural to sit in stillness, go for it. Swimming in the ocean, dancing, walking, cooking, being naked, creating art, making music, are all opportunities for meditation. I love to meditate first thing when I wake up while in bed. Or, I like to take an early morning walk in the woods near my home. So while the location might change, the time is pretty consistent.

Step 2: Set a timer (if you want) for however long you want to practice. Often people will say, "I don't have time to meditate," yet the choice for time is completely up to you. Beginning with five minutes might be the perfect amount of time. You might decide to do ten one-minute meditations throughout the day. Or you might decide that fifteen minutes feels nice, or twenty minutes, or thirty minutes.

Step 3: Take a few deep, clearing breaths as you welcome all of yourself fully to the practice. No matter where you go on your *yatra*, or inner journey, have a friendly attitude with whatever arises. In the authenticity chapter, we began with a short "I welcome" meditation, and that is where we begin this practice. You can simply say, "I welcome all of myself here. I welcome my body, breath, heart, mind; I welcome all of my joy and sadness (and anything that arises)."

Step 4: Choose a doorway to enter. A doorway is the starting point or home base of meditation, and there are infinite doorways you can try. A doorway can be the breath, a mantra, or a specific emotion or feeling. One of the best doorways is each of the senses, because they're always available to you. In traditional meditation you are told what doorway you are supposed to enter (i.e., "focus on your breath"), and that is one reason why so many people don't stick with the practice: they were required to use a doorway that didn't truly interest them.

Another wonderful doorway technique is to use a memory, a word, a song, or the idea of someone in your life that embodies the quality that will generate the feeling you are calling into the meditation. For instance, I've been surfing for about twenty years, and I'm an eternal beginner. I like small waves. One day I was in Hawaii and it was absolutely perfect. The waves were small and manageable. A whale breached nearby. I just felt radiant. I felt so alive, I felt so healthy, I felt beautiful, I felt glowing. That's a memory I often return to as my doorway.

Step 5: Allow yourself to enjoy the rhythm of rest and activity, of being with your chosen doorway and the moments when you journey away. There will be moments when you are immersed in the doorway in which you began, and moments when you feel you have gone somewhere else. Remember, *prana*, the powerful life force that runs through you, is intelligent and is actually on your side. If you find that your mind is "away" from the doorway you entered, the intelligence of *pranashakti* is probably healing or acting—and this is a good thing. And if you are in a place other than where you began (you will be!) you simply ask, "What is more interesting—do I want to tend to whatever has arisen (the ache in my heart, the to-do list) *or* do I want to go back into the doorway in which I began?"

Whatever interests you most is your choice. Whatever you choose, let it guide your meditation. You might say to yourself, "I'm going to hold this emotional wound right now. I'm going to be with this. I'm just going to tend to it, no different than how I would tend to a child or a physical wound. And just simply be with it without shaming any other thoughts that come up. Or, you might say, "Actually, I want to go back into the doorway of sound right now." And then you go back and be with the doorway you began with. Your mind did not wander, it wondered; it is healing, or acting, or repairing, or remembering, or rehearsing.

Wherever you choose to go in the moment, allow yourself to merge with it, be curious about it. Be nourished by the experience of experiencing. This is when you might feel moments of cherishing, melting into, or a deep sense of being held. Yet there is no expectation or guarantee of what's going to happen. We simply want to be welcoming to the entire *yatra*, and allow ourselves to be surprised by what shows up.

Sometimes meditation may feel like magic, and sometimes it will feel mundane. Sometimes meditation might feel like you're daydreaming. Other times it may feel like you are putting together a to-do list for life. Sometimes ruminating in your meditation motivates you to take action. And this is where life is meditation. We're always in this dance, being called into a state of alignment, and integrity, and truth, and we're getting feedback all the time that points to where we are out of alignment, living outside of integrity. And we are pointed toward the moments of being able to fall in love with life.

Step 6: When your allotted time is over, you can end the meditation. It is important to take time to transition: don't rush from your meditation. Give yourself time to savor it. You may want to journal again, do some deep breathing or movement, or find some other way to transition that marks the end of one experience before you move on to another.

ONE DEGREE SHIFT INQUIRY:
Potential Meditation Doorways to Explore

If meditation is yoga and yoga is yoking, or making connections, select something you want to be in relationship with. Instinctive meditation invites the journey to begin by selecting an aspect of *prana* you love, and diving in.

Here are some questions or inquiries to discover which doorway could support you in discovering a meditation practice you will love:

- What do I want to be filled up with? If it were a lotion you would want to lather it all over. If it were an elixir you would want to drink it. Or what aspect of life do you want to be with? It might be peace, love, courage, joy. What are you longing for more of in your life?
- What interests you so much you want to immerse yourself in it?
- What is a feeling you want to be saturated by?
- What is an emotion or thought you want to be with?
- What is the feeling you want to spend time with?
- What object delights you?
- What sense do you want to be with?

What Instinctive Meditation Can Look Like

To give you a better sense of what you might experience, let's explore the sense of sound as a doorway into meditation. Once you are in your preferred position (seated, standing, etc.), begin to notice the sounds nearby. Then, start to notice sounds farther away. From there you would allow yourself to be with all sounds, welcoming everything into the moment. You might be absorbed in this place of "I hear the fan in the room" or "I hear the birds outside" or "I hear my children in the living room." You might feel that you're really marinating in this place of sound. You might think, "I'm connected, I'm aligned, I'm very present." And then the mind goes on a journey. A thought is probably going to pop up, like, "I need to get avocados for dinner tonight." In those moments when your mind is journeying, you can begin to see that meditation is like an adventure. Your to-do list is holy! Being with the sense of sound *and* thinking about avocados is all part of the meditation.

If you notice that you are thinking of the avocado, rather than shaming yourself, or saying, "I must bring my attention back," simply ask yourself, "What is more interesting, the avocado or going back to the doorway of sound where I began?" At this point it would be your choice to explore what is more interesting to you in that moment. What is calling for your attention and care?

After you've made your choice and are in the next moment, you are invited to choose again and then again, and again. There is no right or wrong way to go. Whatever amount of time you've chosen for this practice, staying with the pulse of being with the doorway in which you began, as well as the moments of healing and activity, is the practice.

The Chocolate Meditation

Imagine the best piece of chocolate you could possibly eat. Then allow yourself to hold the chocolate, feel the chocolate, smell the chocolate, and now taste the chocolate. As your lips touch the chocolate you might find you are cherishing the taste of the chocolate. And then in a moment you feel like you have melted into the chocolate and you are overtaken by the deliciousness of the chocolate. Then you and the chocolate have become one for a moment! And then poof, you have journeyed somewhere else away from the chocolate. In that moment, you ask yourself what is more interesting, what do I want to tend to, or what do I want to be with—the chocolate or wherever else the journey has taken you. It is always your choice. That's instinctive meditation.

Meditations to Try

Spending time with your dog, going for a walk, cooking, or dancing may already be your meditation practice. If you are looking for a few more suggestions for doorways, here are my favorites. You may want to record yourself reading these meditation instructions so that you can simply listen to them and meditate:

Meditation #1: *Indriyas:* Delight in the Senses

This meditation focuses on the senses. In yoga teachings, Indra is the king of the gods, and *indriyas* are the senses—sound, touch, smell, taste, and hearing, which are his companions. Indra loves celebrating life and drinking *soma*, the elixir of life, and reminds us that the senses are to be cherished. In this meditation, you will soak in the senses, the indriyas, and drink in the soma through your eyes, ears, nose, skin, and mouth.

Step 1: Find a comfortable position for your body. You are free to move, stretch, or adjust your position at any time.

Step 2: Set your timer to your desired meditation length.

Step 3: Take a few deep, clearing breaths as you welcome all of yourself to this practice. Feel where your body is in contact with the floor, cushion, or chair. Feel your clothing touching your skin. Feel the temperature of air. Feel the subtle movements that your body makes. Feel your breathing.

Step 4: Try the doorway of sound. Rather than reaching or looking for a sound to connect with, be open to sounds that naturally come to you. Maybe you hear the rustling of leaves or a dog barking in the distance. Now sense sounds that are close by . . . sounds that are far away . . . sounds that are short . . . sounds that have a constant hum. Welcome sounds you are drawn toward and sounds you wish were not there.

Step 5: Allow yourself to enjoy the rhythm of rest and activity, of being with sound and the moments when you journey away. Celebrate the entire journey! Enjoy the moments when you are daydreaming, making your to-do list, healing, repairing, rehearsing, or restoring, and enjoy the moment when you are called to choose what is more interesting, and what you want to tend to or be with—such as, do you want to be with your to-do list or the doorway of sound in which you began? Whatever you choose, it is the right way.

Step 6: Now, allow yourself to be with sight. With your eyes open, delight in the colors, shapes, movement, and the art piece that is life itself. What delights your eyes, what are you drawn toward?

Step 7: Again, allow yourself to enjoy the rhythm of rest and activity, of being with sight and the moments when you journey away. Enjoy the moments when you are daydreaming, making your to-do list, healing, repairing, rehearsing, or restoring, and enjoy the moment when you are called to choose what is more interesting, and what you want to tend to or be with—either your to-do list or the doorway of sight in which you began.

Step 8: Continue to explore other senses such as smell, touch, and taste as doorways into meditation.

Step 9: Transition—begin to take a few deep breaths. Feel the quality of your experience. Take a few moments to feel and move your body in any way that feels natural.

Meditation #2: *Pranava:* Celebrate What You Love

Pranava is a nickname for the sacred syllable *om*, and as Lorin says, "Pranava is considered the roar of joy that put the universe into motion and the primordial sound of the universe continually and ecstatically singing itself into existence!"

This meditation invites you into the doorway of that which brings you joy or what you love. This could be an object, a person, or an experience, just like I sometimes use my perfect day of surfing. This could also be a pet, place, poem, song, or memory. Ask yourself, "What object or experience makes me say *oooo, ahhhh, mmmm, haaa*, yes!"

Step 1: Find a comfortable position for your body. You are free to move, stretch, or adjust your position at any time.

Step 2: Set a timer.

Step 3: Take a few deep, clearing breaths, as you welcome all of yourself to this practice.

Step 4: The doorway you are entering is something that brings you joy or that you love. Think of something, someone, or some place you love and would enjoy connecting with. Allow yourself to paint an internal picture of what you love. If it is a person, what does their face look like? Can you see into their eyes, and hear the sound of their voice? How do you feel in their presence? If it is a place, what is the landscape? Are there trees? Flowers? Water? What are the sounds you hear, what do you see? What is around you? How do you feel in this place?

Step 5: Allow the natural rhythm of meditation to occur, of being with what you love and moments when you journey away. Trust there is no right or wrong way to connect with what you love. When your mind is aware of other sensations, thoughts, memories, or is even falling asleep, let it happen.

When you want to be with what you love (the doorway you began with) you naturally will—so just let it happen. Enjoy the natural rhythm of meditation.

Step 6: Transition—begin to take a few deep breaths. Feel the quality of your experience. Take a few moments to feel and move your body in any way that feels natural.

Meditation #3: Your Personal *Mantra*

A mantra is a string of words woven together that resonates with you and which you say out loud or to yourself. Your mantra is usually a word or a phrase that lights you up and supports you in feeling more connected. You can think of your mantra as music for your inner life and nutrition for your soul.

Step 1: Find a comfortable position. You may even want to try this one standing; you might find that your body wants to move with the mantra.

Step 2: Set a timer.

Step 3: Take a few deep, clearing breaths as you welcome all of yourself to this practice.

Step 4: The doorway for this meditation is a mantra. Choose a phrase that you want to fill yourself with. Something you long for, a feeling you crave, or an energy you want to infuse yourself with. It might be peace, passion, strength, courage, grace. For example, "I am connected. I am safe. I create healthy boundaries." Repeat your mantra out loud or to yourself. You might find that your mantra changes during the meditation. Welcome any changes and let yourself be surprised by what shows up.

Step 5: Allow the natural rhythm of meditation to occur. There will be moments you are with your mantra, and moments you have journeyed somewhere else—you may be healing, repairing, relaxing, or reviewing. If it becomes more interesting to be with your mantra again, you naturally will, there is nothing to force!

Step 6: When the meditation is complete, allow yourself a few minutes to transition.

Meditation is much sweeter when it is something you look forward to, not something you feel obliged to do. And if you find you are looking forward to meditation, that's how you will know it is working. You may also find that you function better in your everyday life. You may be better able to be with all the waves of life, or feel more alive and intimate with life. You may feel like your life makes more sense, not that it's more confusing. For me, this practice allowed me to open up to the vast mystery of the universe, to soften and delight in all the wonders of life.

The Radiance Sutras ends with what is referred to as the Insight Verses, and reminds us that accessing the divine is always available, and that there are infinite doorways to the divine that is infusing everything, everywhere. This verse reminds me that instinctive meditation is a practice of wonder and delight. It allows me to fully offer my heart to the practice. It is why we refer to this practice as one of intimacy, and connecting to what you love.

Adorable Goddess,
These practices are a nectar I share with you.
Drink from this cup whenever you are thirsty
Or crave to be refreshed in the essence of life.

Know that this ambrosia is available to you
Everywhere, for the universe is made out of it.
Simply go to the intersection of flesh and spirit,
Breathe the tiny sparks that fly.

Within this very body
Are many gateways to the infinite,
Where incarnation and immortality
Consummate their passion for each other.

from *The Radiance Sutras*

7

The Power of Pause

A pause,
where infinity resides,
and possibilities are created.

We have glorified being busy. When we're trying as hard as we can to get somewhere, we often miss what is right in front of us: a new opportunity, the kindness of a friend, or even our health and vitality. Even in the moments when we have space to rest and recharge, like when we are on vacation, or on the weekends, we continue to work, fill our free time by tackling our to-do lists, or make too many commitments.

All this activity can be exhausting and depleting, and can leave us feeling burned out and overextended. Worse, without leaving time for self-care, we are less likely to be able to cherish the gift of life, skillfully ride the waves, and perform to our greatest potential. And, when we have pushed ourselves to our limits, we can act out of habit rather than aligning with our empowered self, and we can make life-depleting choices or see our lives through distorted lenses. Or the epidemic of comparison takes over and invites the gremlins in, especially the ones that say, "Do more!" In these moments the waves of life can seem unmanageable.

Feeling drained not only impacts our inner landscape; it affects our ability to show up for others and for our community. When life gets busy it can be challenging to feel connected to our deepest self and have awareness for the needs of others. When we continue to go, go, go, our minds can feel like a boisterous windstorm, or excessive noise or unending activity. This inner noise makes it difficult to truly listen—to ourselves and to those we care about.

The Magic of Pause

Sometimes we can get caught on autopilot, yet in yoga we are invited to welcome all of the rhythms of life. The Sanskrit word *shoni* can mean to slow down. When you slow down you are able to experience more and have a deeper reverence for the mystery and the intricacy of life. When we slow down we are able to live a more conscious and deliberate life. Slowing down could be the one degree shift that could change the course of your life.

The easiest way to slow down is to put your mental brakes on and simply pause, even for a second. A pause can be a deliberate practice of non-doing: it is the choice not to act. It can be the dynamic stillness that exists in a hovering breath or the expansive space of relaxation. It can be prolonged time away or a brief moment to reset. When you slow down and pause, you take a break from what you are doing and make space for rest, healing, creativity, awareness, or whatever it is you are craving more of to arise. A pause allows for choice—to make a shift, to see things more clearly. It creates a moment for *involution*, a time of turning our attention to ourselves so that we can slow down, rest, and reflect.

Though the mind is designed to problem-solve and be the command center for the body's basic functions, it can become challenging to focus and direct our intention and attention if we don't regularly pause. A pause could be a single breath, a break from a conversation, or a break in a relationship. It can be a break from work, or at times a break from doing the work. A pause could be a weekend away or a sabbatical. A pause could be a nap, the moments lingering in bed in the morning listening to the birds, or carving out time to write a poem or write creative thoughts down on paper.

Almost every September I take some time off and pause from what I think is "true" to make sure I still believe it. I don't work or teach at all during this time—I use this period to put aside everything I think, teach, and believe to check in with myself and make sure I still resonate with it, and that it hasn't just become a habit—or just what I automatically say when I teach. I allow myself to step into a beginner's mind—to see with fresh eyes. I use this time to rest and recharge. I use this time to ask, Who am I really? I use this time to reflect. I use this time to have gratitude for my life. I pause during this time to simply allow there to be space—for creativity, for writing letters (yes, handwritten letters). I pause so I can check in with what is trying to get my attention. I pause to savor simply being. I pause to do nothing.

But not all pauses are created equally. Though there may be a time and place for TV, happy hour, and eating out, these moments that seem like they are pauses from our daily responsibilities and routines, when overused, can actually deplete us rather than provide the space to reboot and rejuvenate. The best way to find out what kind of pause would serve you best is to put yourself into the experiment. There isn't a right or wrong, as one form of pause might work better during a certain moment or season of your life while another might be a better fit at another time. Changing the types of pauses you take might be your one degree shift.

For instance, I tend to spend a lot of my pauses in nature, journaling, or in some kind of inward reflection—where I can end up going down my own rabbit hole and turn into an existential detective! Though I love this part of myself, it can also be exhausting. Sometimes, I just need to pause and watch a funny movie, and be with the joy and lightness it brings, which can lead me to more inspiration and fuel so that I can feel inspired to do the existential work.

Pause to Connect

When we take time to pause, we are invited to connect, and to be more connected. Connected to the ground. Connected to your creativity. Connected to your power. Connected to your passion. Connected to your heart. Connected to your voice. Connected to your intuition. Connected to another person. Connected to grace. Connected to remembering what really matters to you and your values. Connected to nature. Connected to your empowered self. Connected to a cause. Connected to your breath.

ONE DEGREE SHIFT INQUIRY:
Walk and Pause

Slow your pace so that each footstep is a conscious choice. Pause between each step and simply notice. Pause and listen to the crunching of the ground beneath your feet, pause and notice the wind brushing the leaves, or the birds singing. Pause and have gratitude for your feet, for the ability to walk, for the earth beneath you.

Pause to Thoughtfully Respond Rather Than React

Yoga invites us to fall in love with all of life and to participate in its unfolding. When we pause we are invited to deeply listen to what is calling for attention. Without it, we might keep re-creating patterns that are not really working, and lose sight of what actually has meaning for us. If there's no pause, we can get stuck in the cycle of continuously reacting to life, rather than thoughtfully responding. Worse, our instant reactions can be informed by our past hurts or wounds, old triggers—the dams that have been created inside of us rather than the issue that is right in front of us.

Pausing to see life clearly also allows you to practice discernment and recognize the difference between habits and true urges. One of the challenges we face is choosing how to respond to difficult situations. Too often, we don't evaluate our response until *after* the moment has passed. When we slow down a situation, pause before we act or speak, we are more able to be in the moment and thoughtfully engage with our actions and words. Of course, pausing after a situation can be useful, to clean up any messes we may have created—and wouldn't it be lovely if we all could pause *before* we acted—to decrease the likelihood of needing to clean something up later?

The pause invites in awareness and allows you to notice where your reaction may have originated from. This creates more opportunity to make a one degree shift, recognize the habit, see where you are stuck in the riptide, and create an opening for change. As you check in with yourself, you can make sure your motivation isn't coming from a story you created. You can ask yourself, "Am I looking at this situation through an old lens? Is this me reliving an old story? Is this me dragging the past into the future?"

In the pause you can respond *to* the moment, rather than react *in* the moment, by inviting your empowered self to show up. For example, if you want to quit your job, or snap at someone who speaks to you in a way you don't like, before you act, pause. Give yourself enough time to connect to what feels real and true. Then, see if you can come back to the question, "Are your words an improvement upon silence?" In other words, are you skillfully responding to the situation? Ask yourself, "What impact will my words or actions have here? Will I feel more alive if I do this? Would my action make the world a friendlier place?"

If the answer to the last two questions is no, then you have the ability to make a shift and respond differently in that moment—and that shift truly could change your life and be the inspiration for others to shift as well.

Pause for Social Silence

Practice social silence—taking a break from speaking, verbally and nonverbally (think: you don't need to smile at everyone who walks by). Experiment by taking in a silent meal, walk in nature on your own, or spend an entire day by yourself to experience what shifts in the presence of silence. This last one is my favorite kind of pause.

Pause to Strengthen Your Witness

The process of slowing down and pausing can also allow us to awaken our witness consciousness or our empowered observer, the part of yourself that has the ability to witness your inner world with compassion. The witness is an ally in the inquiry of life, allowing you to observe your inner and outer landscape with a clearer gaze and to make more empowered choices from that place. Through this observation, you begin to develop a stronger relationship with yourself and, ultimately, a more intimate and freer relationship with the dance of life. Creating a strong witness allows us to more easily be with whatever comes up, to stay present and adapt to whatever circumstance arises, and to say yes to life in all of its complexities and forms. The witness helps us to notice our feelings, sensations, and thoughts without reacting, and, from that place, we can respond with choices that better serve us. And if we do react, we can recognize this more quickly and are better able to clean up that situation with integrity and ease. This skill of stepping back and observing can serve us in both our personal and professional lives as it invites us to be aware of and sensitive to what's going on around us.

By taking more time in your life to pause—whether it be a few deep breaths, a five-minute meditation, or a refreshing walk in nature, you begin to set yourself up to be more successful in responding to life as you strengthen your relationship with your witness consciousness. Meditation, in particular, can be a time that you carve out of your day to go into your inner world and go on your inner journey, a pause from the busyness of life.

When you pause, parts of yourself that you might have shied away from or lost contact with might begin to resurface. You might also begin to notice more clearly the self-limiting beliefs and habitual patterns that don't serve you. When I was younger, my mom used to say to me, "It's what you don't know, that you don't know, that can really hurt you." As you practice and flex this muscle of awareness, you can have a more conscious and deliberate relationship with the choices of daily life. You can recognize where you're out of alignment. You can recognize where you're creating crimes against wisdom. You can recognize when you're more interested in being right than being in relationship—the times when we fight to be right rather than staying in the conversation and navigating a relationship we cherish.

ONE DEGREE SHIFT INQUIRY:
Pause for Awareness

The practice is to simply pause and invite in awareness by activating witness consciousness. Nothing to analyze, nothing to do, just pause and notice.

Put yourself in a place where you can sit for a few minutes. Allow yourself to pause and notice what is going on around you. As you become attuned to what you notice, simply say out loud (or to yourself) exactly what you are aware of. Continue for a full five minutes. Use your emotional responses and all of your senses for this exploration:

- I am aware that I see...
- I am aware that I smell...
- I am aware that I hear...
- I am aware that I feel...
- I am aware of...

Sometimes People Pause for Too Long

Some people let their fears or gremlins get in the way of taking action, and end up pausing for too long. They think that if they pause just a little while longer they can gather more data, or that the situation will resolve itself on its own. Yet this is not always the case. There is a difference between deliberately pausing and playing it safe by sitting on the sidelines of life.

By strengthening your witness consciousness, you can figure out if you pause too long because of your fears or gremlins. If that is your typical reaction, put yourself in the experiment: What would it be like for you to say "yes" rather than saying "let's wait and see?"

A pause isn't an excuse. Don't watch life pass you by. Be daring to take the risk and respond. Sometimes you need to leave, quit, or just jump. You might be surprised by a deep sense of relief, freedom, or the joy that comes with that kind of change.

Pause to Savor

Yoga invites us to savor the life that is happening right here. When we are invested in fully savoring life we have the ability to experience more sweetness, a natural intoxication, and beauty in the day-to-day. Even as you read these pages, are you truly *reading* them, or just rushing through? Pause and be in awe that you know how to read, that somehow, what I am trying to convey you are absorbing. Isn't that amazing! Pause and be amazed.

It's normal to think of the past or daydream about the future, but when you spend most of your life *there* and not *here*, something can be lost. So many people are trying to get *there*, and if they just paused for a moment they might realize that what they were seeking over *there* was actually right *here*. By pausing we are able to enhance our intimacy with life because the moments slow down and we are able to digest the experiences as they are unfolding.

The word *madhuri* can mean sweetness, and teaches that the sweetness of life is ever present. Just like the bee collects nectar from different flowers and then brings them to the hive to get processed, our life is the gathering of various experiences. Part of the magic of pausing is giving time to a situation whether it was easy or challenging, and to discover the sweetness that is present within it.

Another aspect of pausing to become more intimate with life is *soma*, or a natural intoxication. So often people are relying on drugs and alcohol to become intoxicated with life. Soma teaches us that if we pause long enough we can become naturally intoxicated with the wonder-filled and majestic world around us. This can happen by being fully present with anything: being in awe of a waterfall, a butterfly, a conversation, an intimate pleasure, or a travel adventure. The world is constantly offering herself to us. Are we simply walking by and ignoring what is before us, or do we also take time out to fully dive in and drink what we are experiencing?

Sundari can mean beauty, and reminds us that we can see splendor in every moment or situation, from a baby being born to the deepest heartbreak, your child going off to college, retirement, or an intense rainstorm. Sundari also shows up when we are truly seeing the world around us. Making eye contact with another person, seeing a pattern from nature, or noticing the beauty of a piece of art. Being in nature can be one of the most nourishing ways to savor beauty and also experience sweetness and natural intoxication. I love to take what I call beauty or wonder walks. As I leisurely stroll (why the rush, slow it down!), I will pause and be with whatever catches my attention. It may last as long as a breath, a minute, or an hour!

ONE DEGREE SHIFT INQUIRY:
Savoring Each Day

Take a thirty-minute solo walk (with no electronics) and try to see your world through the lens of sweetness and beauty. What do you see that is new for you? What is the relationship between sweetness, beauty, and a natural intoxication? Journal about your experience when you return.

Pause for Gratitude

Taking time to pause for gratitude is such a simple yet profound shift because it works. I know you have heard it, tried it, and forgotten to do it. And, I promise you, you want to bring it back into your life.

Too often, we focus on all of our problems—and yes, we all know there are so many things that should be fixed. At the same time, our lives are filled with miracles and beauty if we could just pause long enough to see. Regardless of your current situation, there is always something to be grateful for.

Years ago, I decided to take a pause each day and write down one thing I was grateful for (and that I loved or appreciated) in my partner. I kept all my thoughts in a journal, diligently recording them every day for an entire year, and when it was over, I gave him this book. This one small pause changed the way I saw him and increased our connection, and was also a gift for him to realize all the ways in which I saw him and was grateful for him.

You don't need to keep a journal or make a scrapbook; you could simply pause and tell someone why you are grateful for them. Or you could pause and have gratitude for waking up today, being able to breathe and walk, having a roof over your head, or the rich supportive relationships you have in your life.

Pause to Celebrate

Now, I don't mean pause and throw a party (unless you want to!), but I do mean pause and celebrate yourself. This has been a lesson that I have had to learn. I never took the time to pause and celebrate completing graduate school, or the victories I have had professionally or personally. Instead, I glazed over them and quickly moved on to whatever was calling me next. Eventually I realized that not taking a pause and honoring the journey I have been on was actually a disservice to all of the effort and dedication I had put in.

Now, I pause and acknowledge my accomplishments, both large and small, and reflect the ways in which I continue to grow and evolve.

Pause to Play

Lila is a Sanskrit word that can mean play, amusement, or pastime, and is often described as the divine play of the universe, in the sense that the universe simply wants to experience itself in all of its different forms and savor the immense diversity. It can also be described as a child playing with a dollhouse; the child is both the director and actor of the dolls—having them speak, play, and engage in different ways. Usually when people think of play, they think of its joyful aspects, like freedom, dancing, or games. From a yogic perspective, lila also teaches that play—and life to some extent—can be random, not personal or deliberate.

If we adopt this idea of lila, we can soften our grip on the idea that everything has to be so serious all the time. Yes, there is a time for seriousness, yet there is also a time for enjoyment. No matter how busy your life is, you can pause for play, even for just a few minutes. A pause can allow you to take a momentary break from adulting, from responsibilities, from the to-do list. You might step out of your daily grind and read a book that makes you laugh, play a board game, learn to play a new instrument, join a sports team, learn to trapeze (one of my favorites), spend time watching comedy, or just let yourself laugh and lighten up!

ONE DEGREE SHIFT INQUIRY:
Make Time to Play

- Where and why have I stopped playing?
- Where am I taking life too seriously?
- What are a few simple ways I can invite more play into the next week of my life?

Pause to Integrate

We have lost the art of marinating, taking the time to completely soak in an experience, and to integrate what we've just learned. Too often we are on to the next thing before we actually experience whatever is calling our attention. It's like we half bake the cake and then eat it. We don't pause long enough for it to cook completely, whether it is an idea, a lesson, or a phase of life.

A pause gives us the time to fully integrate and embody an experience. It can allow knowledge to turn into wisdom, or a practice to turn into insight. This one degree shift means "going deep" and fully exploring a single experience rather than "going wide" and getting a surface appreciation for many different experiences.

ONE DEGREE SHIFT INQUIRY:
Using Breath to Pause

How could you include a pause today, even if it is for a minute, an hour, or for the entire day? Rather than filling the space with anything, could you just pause and do nothing?

One quick pause to try is to notice the magic that happens between an inhale and exhale. Bring awareness to the air that gives you life. Take a moment to give thanks for the life flowing in and out of you with each breath. When you inhale and sustain the breath in or exhale and hover the breath out, it's like the inhale craves the exhale, and the exhale craves the inhale. They are flirting with each other.

• Sit tall and engage in several rounds of full yogic breathing (see chapter 3 for instructions).

- Close your right nostril (with right thumb) and slowly inhale through the left nostril for a count of four.
- Finish inhaling, pause for a count of four, and notice what you feel as you pause.
- Gently close your left nostril (with the ring finger and pinky finger) and exhale through the right nostril for a count of four.
- Finish exhaling, pause for a count of four, and notice what you feel as you pause, and then inhale through your right nostril for a count of four.
- Finish inhaling, pause for a count of four, and notice what you feel as you pause.
- Close your right nostril and exhale through the left for a count of four.
- Continue this pattern for a few minutes and then finish by letting go of the technique and returning to a natural breath.
- Pause and notice what you feel.

Pause to Rest and Heal

Another gift of pausing is to receive the benefits of rest. When we keep pushing and pushing and never truly let the body rest, it is unable to fully heal. Nature rests during winter or when animals go into hibernation, and we too as a part of this natural rhythm need moments of rest as well. Whether you are in need of physical, emotional, or spiritual healing, pausing provides the opportunity to rejuvenate. You don't need to take a nap every day (although you could) but even a few minutes to take a few deep breaths, or put your legs up the wall can create a container for healing. When we pause we can provide the body time to repair, renew, and give us the simple pleasure of a deep exhale. At least for a moment.

ONE DEGREE SHIFT INQUIRY:
Legs up the Wall

This restorative yoga posture allows for deep relaxation. It allows your body to work with gravity and allows the ground to support you. Many people find this to be extremely nourishing and restful.

- Lie down on the floor with your buttocks against the wall. Straighten your legs so that the bottom of your feet are facing the ceiling. Keep your spine perpendicular to the wall, your neck supported, your throat open, and your shoulders relaxed. Take time to set up this posture so that your body can release deeply and be in a configuration free of kinks and obstructions. If your hamstrings feel overly contracted and your lower back is in tension, move your buttocks slightly away from the wall and bend your knees a bit.
- Cover your eyes (an eye pillow or washcloth work great). Let your hands rest on your lower abdomen and feel the movement of your breath drop down into your palms. Encourage your breath to be rhythmic and to flow naturally while you simply allow it to be, without guidance or control.
- Stay in the pose for five to fifteen minutes. Keep your

attention on your breath and the feelings in your body. A little bit of coolness or a tingly sensation is normal. If your legs start to feel overly drained or uncomfortably tingly, release the posture.

- To exit the pose, bend your knees and bring the soles of your feet against the wall. Rest here for a few breaths, then roll onto your side and shift your bottom arm to support your head. Lie on your side until you feel that your blood pressure has normalized—getting up too quickly could result in lightheadedness or even blacking out.

Pause to Read the Field

Have you ever walked into a room and felt its energy? Have you been to a yoga studio that feels peaceful, or a concert that feels electrifying? Imagine you walk in on two people who just had an argument, though they are not arguing anymore—you can sense that something is off. The mood in a space can be referred to as the *bhav*, which in yoga is usually described as the emotion or mood conveyed by a performer. If you can pick up on the bhav, the vibe, mood, or feel of a physical space, you are "reading the field," and getting a greater sense for what is going on. By doing so, you can have a better idea as to how you can contribute or affect change.

Every field has a different feeling to it, depending on who is there and what is being created. The field can be any space created between two people, a room, or even a community. Our collective consciousness impacts the field and gives it its energy. This is how we define a period of time, by giving it a voice. The voices that are speaking out are shaping the field. In the 1960s the country could no longer ignore the anti-war movement, and today, we can no longer ignore the political divide, social injustices, and the impact we are having on the planet.

The ability to read the field is an art. There is no exact science or rule book on how to do it. Reading the field allows us to assess a situation by taking a step back and even removing our perspective or bias and allowing ourselves to witness, observe, and check in with our intuition on what we sense is going on.

When you have the ability to pause and read the field you are more likely to skillfully act. You can get a better understanding of what is actually needed from you, and what will most positively impact the space. It allows you to see if there is anything that seems like it needs to be energetically cleaned up. Does the field need some attending to? Is there something not being said that needs to be addressed? Sometimes when I am teaching I can sense that the field needs a movement break, or some humor to lighten the mood, or time for reflection.

My belief is that an amazing facilitator, leader, partner, or friend takes the time to pause and read the field and is willing to experiment with how to tend to it. For example, I was once offered a job to work as a business coach for a national executive coaching company. The CEO flew me across the country so I could participate in a staff-wide training.

During the training I kept quiet at first and just watched what was going on around me. I quickly noticed that the energy in the room was resistant to the facilitator who was leading the training. When I paused and read the field, I could clearly sense a feeling of mistrust. The facilitator didn't appear to be picking up on this feeling, and I could see that he had lost his audience. Rather than just jumping in right away, I paused again and watched the situation unfold. Finally, I felt an urge to respond, and said, "I know I'm brand new to this company. It seems to me like something else is going on in this room that's not being said. What's the elephant in the room? Would it be beneficial to check in?"

As soon as I stopped talking it was like Pandora's box had opened, and you could feel the relief in the room. The CEO chimed in and said, "You're right, Coby, we need to tend to our affairs." At the end of the day, the CEO said to me, "I imagine you don't want to work here now." I responded, "I actually do, because the fact that you would let go of your original agenda to allow for what was needed in the field, to me, was a moment of true leadership."

Pausing and reading the field was key for making that particular day successful. We are all invited into the practice of combining a pause with conscious communication, regardless of our status, role, or position. Sometimes we can misread the field—we can be looking at a situation through a distorted lens or from the perspective of our gremlins. That's why it is so important to pause, check in, and maybe even pause again before you jump to conclusions.

ONE DEGREE SHIFT INQUIRY:
Reading the Field

Reading the field works best when you put your personal feelings aside and get a sense of the collective mood. Again, it will never be that everyone in an entire group or space (or field) will all feel the same thing at the same time; it is simply the ability to sense the overall vibe.

- How does the field in the space you are in feel right now? Does it feel peaceful, hostile, energetic, or inclusive?

  ◦ What about your workplace?

> ○ Your relationship?
>
> ○ The community you live in?
>
> ○ The country you live in?
>
> • Would the field you are in right now benefit if it shifted?
>
> • How could you impact the field you are in right now? What is one small shift you could make to potentially shift the field?

Unplug and Pause

So many people are absorbed in their tech devices, even while they are walking, that they miss so much of their present. To navigate the amount of time technology eats up, I've set up an automatic reply for emails that come in. It reads: "Dear Friend, I have limited email access and will do my best to reply to your message. If you have not heard from me within three weeks, please feel free to email me again."

I get many different reactions from people about this statement, ranging from frustration to envy. However, for me, this message sets up the expectation that I can take a pause from technology if and when I want to. Technology is great, don't get me wrong, but when it's used without focus and intention, it can be draining. Too often people say how busy they are, and by simply cutting your online time in half, that could be a one degree shift that could change your life.

ONE DEGREE SHIFT INQUIRY:
Digital Detox

Choose a time or a day of the week to unplug from all devices and do a digital detox. Discover what is possible when you take a break/pause from your devices.

- How did you feel when you unplugged?
- How did that feeling change?
- How much time did it take for the feeling to change?
- What is the value of doing a digital detox? What becomes available?

Making Pause a Ritual

When I was teaching and traveling in India I was deeply moved by a daily ritual, or *puja*, that many people performed. Puja can be translated as reverence, adoration, or worship. Often a puja would include a mantra; an honoring of *agni*, the element of fire; and an offering of some kind, such as food, garlands of flowers, water, or candles.

These rituals inspired me to create my own type of puja. I try to pause at the start of my day (or any time to recognize special moments, such as a new year, the new moon, or new beginnings) and sit at my altar, where I use crystals, essential oils, flowers, and candles, and recite a mantra as a way to honor the moment. Yoga teaches that each moment is rare and that there is impermanence to life. My morning pause allows me to soak in this moment, have gratitude, and savor.

Nature also has lessons to teach, and is, as I have mentioned, where I most often take a pause. You might have heard the phrase "forest bathing"—taking time to receive the healing qualities of nature. I take time most days to be with nature, to pause and savor in its silence. I leave all devices at home, walk slowly to breathe, feel, and allow life to move through me with no agenda.

Another way I love to connect to nature as a way of pausing is creating art from what nature has left on the earth. Sometimes this is referred to as earth art or forest paintings. It's quite a simple yet beautiful practice. Take time to quietly be in nature, forage what is on the ground—leaves, rocks, flower petals, acorns, pine cones (avoid taking anything that hasn't already "fallen")—and find some space outdoors to take what you have collected. Creating forest art can be an activity as well as a meditation. Using what you find on your walk, make a piece of art and leave it behind as a way to practice impermanence. I have seen people create a *mandala*—often described as a geometric shape or circle that represents the universe. Simply let this be a time of pausing, connecting with nature, the impermanence of life, the gifts of the earth, and the reminder of beauty that is all around—and the art piece that *is* life.

Pause,
and
receive the boons of life.
Embrace motion
rather than imposing stillness,
and feel the settling
that happens naturally.
Without effort,
with ease.
Pause and feel the current of love that
pulses through

your body,
that moves the essence of who you are.
A dance of body and breath into a
sea of ecstatic stillness.
Know with this simple pause, you have taken the first step
that leads you to the temple of infinity.

Rewriting Your Story

You are not your past.
You are not your wounds.
You are the co-creator of your reality.

❧

t's not surprising that our worldview and the different ways we think about ourselves are shaped both by the specific events that have occurred in our lives and the beliefs that have been passed on to us by our parents and relatives, as well as the collective conscious-ness, or cultural context. Yet just because we have ideas about the world, how life operates, our self-image, and how we fit into the big picture, it doesn't mean that these thoughts are particularly accurate. In many cases, we've adopted a point of view about ourselves that doesn't serve us. In fact, sometimes these thoughts are what make us feel stuck. Or, we are looking at one part of life through a lens that was created by a belief or perspective that isn't ours, and isn't congruent to the rest of our beliefs; it's as if we're looking at life through someone else's prescription glasses.

Yoga refers to this distorted perspective as *maya*, or the cosmic illusion. It is said that maya is a creative force that can keep us from seeing the interconnectedness of life. When we get stuck in our own subjective reality we can lose perspective and get overly attached to a singular viewpoint of how the world should look and function. We are looking through the lens of maya when we can't see beyond our own narratives and limiting beliefs. The more these illusions take root, the more they block us from living life from an authentic and caring place.

Yoga is defined by some as the ability to see life clearly, without fear, fantasy, or distortion: to see into the illusions that are not serving our life vitality. In order to do this, we are invited into the inquiry of *om tat sat*, which refers to seeking what is real and true. This journey of stepping into Truth and Reality for some *is* the true quest of yoga.

For some yoga practitioners, om tat sat is the ultimate inquiry, although it doesn't have to be yours. I believe that the journey is not about getting to the end of the road; it's having the ability to see where you've been and to trust the unfolding of your life—moment by moment, step by step. This does not have to be your ultimate aim, but it can be! And, if it's not, just taking one step in that direction will create a new space in your life: this inquiry of om tat sat can be the one degree shift that could change the course of your life. It is the ability to shift beliefs that keep you in a state of illusion or delusion (maya), which will help you separate the past from the present, so that you can move toward a brighter future that is free from the confines of your past. This inquiry of what is true and real, and cutting through these distortions, invites you to have a healthier relationship with life. With a better understanding of what is true and real, you can both honor your unique path and dare to rewrite your story: to keep the beliefs that are helpful and transform the ones that are not, so that you can step into co-creating the next chapter of your life.

Two of my favorite expressions are the phrases "historically speaking" and "up until this point." I use them when I see people drag their past into the present and let it affect their future. When I remind myself that "historically" I used to believe something, or acted in a certain way, it leaves space for me to evolve and create change in the future. For example, you may have a fear of speaking in public. Instead of assuming that you will always be terrified, you could say to yourself, "Up until this point I have been terrified of speaking in public," or, "Historically speaking, I was terrified of speaking in public, but let's see what is true today."

The truth is, your story, your beliefs, and your frame of reference is yours for the making. By revisiting these beliefs, and testing out if they actually work for you, you may finally be able to let go of past hurts or old wounds. Then you can use the truth to improve your life and the lives of others.

In some ways this journey is like *Alice's Adventures in Wonderland*. You are entering into the rabbit hole—into a world of wonder and curiosity. To see beyond maya, one must be willing to be open to the fact that we simply don't know everything that is going on—and maybe, just maybe, we can start to shift the course of our life by letting go of the old beliefs that no longer serve us.

ONE DEGREE SHIFT INQUIRY:
What Are Your Beliefs?

Believe it or not, your beliefs are impacting the way you both view and experience life. So let's check in and see what you believe to be true.

This exercise is meant to be quick; you are collecting data about your actual beliefs, not what you think you are supposed to believe. These are ten topics to explore; know that there are many more you might benefit from looking more deeply into, as they are most likely also impacting your life. Other topics could include your beliefs around government, sexuality, religion, the environment, or food.

Without thinking too much, write down just one belief you have about each of the following, and any additional topics you want to check in on:

1. Your body
2. Your self-worth
3. Cancer
4. Love
5. Relationships
6. Money
7. Death
8. Drugs
9. Your story
10. Your ability to manifest/create what you want

The next step is to review the list again, and ask yourself, "Are these beliefs helpful or not? Are they serving my highest self? Do they support the life I want to live, make me feel more alive and connected? Do they align with my authentic self?"

If these beliefs are helpful, that's great: stick with them! And if you can point to some beliefs that clearly aren't helpful or supportive, you are now invited to challenge or shift these beliefs, and get curious as to why you are holding on to them.

When the Inner Rivers Stop Flowing

Remember the *nadis*—the energetic rivers or channels that are designed to remain open and flowing, and can become blocked due to life experiences and the imprints we carry from our childhood, including heartbreaks and fears. Holding on to beliefs that keep us stuck can prevent us from freely engaging with life: they create dams or blockages in the energetic rivers which can distort what we think is real and true, and can lead to us to construct beliefs that don't serve us. Our daily obligations often mean that we are riding lots of diverse waves at the same time. Whether we're navigating family and children, school and jobs, or bills and mortgages, these responsibilities can also create stress and tension that drain our energy and prevent it from flowing. That's not a bad thing; it's just the nature of life itself. Sometimes we move with ease, and sometimes we get clogged up.

Sometimes, when we create a block in the flow, a story or belief gets coupled with the experience that happened. These dams can create stagnation, and can lead us to fester and focus on some part of our lives that ultimately makes us feel disconnected from ourselves or others. As a result, we might become dissatisfied with life and feel anxious or even depressed. These stories can often be the fuel or evidence of our gremlins and can include themes like "I'm not lovable"; "I'm not special"; "I'm not good enough"; "The world is a scary place"; "I'm always going to be alone." Then, as time goes on we start collecting evidence that these beliefs are true and the fog of illusion starts to set in and we fester even more.

Any thought, belief, or habit can become a *samskara*, which means a fixed routine, or a groove or impression. Think about a well-preserved fossil, where you can clearly see its detailed features. Just like a fossil, when the energetic rivers or channels get a dam and a samskara is created, we get stuck in an emotional groove that creates a lasting impression. These grooves create habits, and we can start to function on autopilot without any awareness. We repeat the same thoughts and take the same actions, over and over again. Sometimes they are useful as in habits that increase our health and feeling of well-being, and other times they can lead us to feel mediocre, afraid, or dissatisfied.

Here's an example: When I was in junior high, I was the only one of my friends who had never kissed a boy. I'd never had a boyfriend and I thought I was never going to. My best friend was very beautiful, and she always got attention from boys. Anytime a boy talked to me, it was always to ask, "Who's your friend? Can I talk to her?" Over time I started to create a story that I wasn't beautiful, and then spent a lot of time collecting data that supported this false narrative.

On one particular day at the Dunkin' Donuts parking lot (yes, this is where fun happens in eastern Massachusetts), an older boy came up to me. He said, "Hey, Coby, I have something to tell you." I was nervous and giddy with excitement that a boy was actually paying attention to me, until he said, "Have you ever read the story *The Ugly Duckling*? I just wanted to let you know that you are the Ugly Duckling, and you're never going to be a beautiful swan."

My heart felt like it broke, my head was spinning, and I was swallowing back the tears. As a twelve-year-old, it seemed like the worst thing I could have ever heard. I took his words as fact. Instantly, my story that I wasn't beautiful was verified, and I added a new chapter: no one was ever going to love me. I carried this story with me for years, until I finally began rewriting my story.

Too often, people struggle because they are looking at their life through this kind of distortion. They hold on to their story and the supporting data because it's all they know, and they have gotten stuck in a way of thinking that further supports that story. For me, I started to believe that external beauty was the most important factor for finding love. It was harder to believe that this hurtful comment was just one boy's perspective, and that it wouldn't hold true in future interactions with other men.

Living yoga reminds us that sometimes the key to freedom is challenging beliefs that create a sense of imprisonment. Transformation can occur when we carve out a new path and let our energy flow in a new direction. Once we can observe the dams created by the wounds and the hurts, we become empowered—because once there is awareness there can be a choice to challenge and then shift the false beliefs.

Another useful tool in this process is to employ compassion with what we observe, because simply in this act of radical self-kindness something is going to shift. Through the observation, we can make different choices and see more clearly what is true and real. As I was learning the lessons in this book and put myself into these same experiments, I wondered, "What is more true than the belief that I am not beautiful? Is it possible that I was looking through a distorted lens?" The inquiry provided my one degree shift when I recognized that I have the power to challenge beliefs and to try on new beliefs—and that trying on the belief that I am beautiful, that I do deserve to be loved, and that I am valuable carried more weight than the belief I took on from that hurtful comment at twelve years old. And this is key: beneath the surface of our false narratives there always resides something that is truer, which can liberate us if we give it attention, and that is more important than the beliefs or hurtful acts of others.

ONE DEGREE SHIFT INQUIRY:
A Samskara Inquiry

When we pause and look at a situation, particularly one where we feel stuck or uncomfortable, we can ask if our perspective is attached to an old story, impression, or *samskara*.

- Where are you living in the past?
- How is living in the past impacting your ability to clearly see what is real and true?
- Is it possible that you are looking through a distorted lens?
- What is the hurt associated with your false narrative?
- Are you still giving away your power to someone or something else that wounded you long ago? What small shift could you make to reclaim your power?
- What is truer than your story, what lies beneath the surface? How might things shift if you embraced that aspect of who you are?

The Story You've Created About Your Life

Though you do not need to relive the pain, sometimes it can be useful to unpack parts of your past and how they have impacted the way you see the world and the story you've created about your life. By writing out and mapping your journey, you can remember influential moments that might have been the beginning few words of your false narrative. By exploring these forgotten experiences you might better be able to bring awareness to the disruptive patterns that show up in the present even though they originated in the past. As you dive more deeply into these stuck ideals and concepts you can recognize the well-etched samskaras that are truly holding you back.

ONE DEGREE SHIFT INQUIRY:
The Timeline of Your Life

Let's go on a journey and see what happened in your life and where some of your beliefs may have been formed. In your journal, draw a line that represents your life. Mark your birth on one end of the timeline and the present moment on the other. Then, revisit in your mind each year and mark down any memorable events. You may want to include words or images to represent your timeline. Get creative!

Once your timeline is complete, divide it into chapters, and give each one its own title. For example, you might say that ages zero to four fall into chapter one and the title is "The Playful Years"; your teen years are part of chapter three and the title could be "Confused and Curious."

After you have labeled each chapter, answer the following questions: From this chapter I...

- Learned...
- Created this belief(s) that was helpful...
- Created this belief(s) that was not helpful...
- Am affected on a daily basis by...

Then, turn back to your timeline and each major milestone, and look at it from the perspective of your empowered, authentic self, then ask the following:

- What advice would you give your younger self? For example, "It's okay to trust people."
- What wisdom do you have for yourself now, based on each different time period? For example, you might tell the twelve-year-old self that you are loveable.
- What do you need to let go of?
- What becomes possible when you look at your timeline with new eyes?

Have Compassion for *All* the Parts of Your Story

There may be parts of your past and your story that you regret, are embarrassed about, feel like you are not able to share with others, or have just completely put out of your memory. Now, I am not saying we need to go around and tell everyone our story, but we also don't need to be ashamed of it. We all have a story. A one degree shift might be that you need support processing parts of your story that seem too difficult to make sense of—this is when your community, or *kula*, can help, including a great therapist or life coach. And it is also possible that with kindness, compassion, and an understanding that you too are learning about life, you can begin to be more gentle and accepting of all parts of your story.

Sometimes, when you start to get honest with yourself, you might notice your gremlins trying to creep in with their judgments—this is a great time to practice creating a boundary with these unkind inner voices. The boundary might be to say to your gremlin, "Thanks for sharing," and then move on to another thought. This technique can help you remember that every comment from your inner voices doesn't deserve or require the same level of attention or care; it doesn't have to carry much weight, especially when it isn't kind.

With a boundary in place it is easier to have more freed-up energy to source compassion. We have all done things that we are not necessarily proud of, but we don't need to define who we are by our past, our mistakes, or our misfortune. Instead we can begin to soften and use kindness for ourselves, which can also lead to a greater level of empathy for others, especially when we recognize how their words and actions might actually be tied back to the false stories they are living from. We are all learning about life, one experience and one moment at a time.

ONE DEGREE SHIFT INQUIRY:
Get Honest with Yourself

The list below is an opportunity for you to get honest with yourself. Circle the statements you have experienced, lived through, felt, or brought upon yourself that may be deemed less than ideal. Again, this is a random list of experiences, or potential life scenarios, and you might benefit from creating a list of other aspects you typically avoid acknowledging. Most everyone will have something on this list or similar, so notice if shame or the thought of "I'm the only one" comes up, and practice letting it go.

As you read the list, if any of the points bring up strong emotions or internal resistance, remember there is power in asking for help and reaching out for support. You don't need to be stuck in the maze; you don't need to feel like you are being held down in the riptide. Reach out to someone because you matter.

1. I have a tattoo I regret.
2. I suffer(ed) from depression and/or anxiety.
3. I have had suicidal thoughts.
4. I have debt greater than $10,000.
5. I have experienced body dysmorphia or an eating disorder.
6. I have been addicted to something.
7. I have an STD.
8. I was abused or I was an abuser.
9. I have cheated.
10. I have stolen something.

Now, take a breath. Sometimes getting more honest with parts of yourself can bring up feelings. You might notice frustration, a desire to push away, sadness or numbness; or maybe you tap into a sense of ease, forgiveness, or zero charge—if you have already integrated some of these past experiences. The power of observation and feeling can provide a shift in itself. If you notice your gremlin creeping in, think of it as another opportunity to practice creating a boundary and inviting in your most authentic self—full of kindness and compassion. The practice is to simply get honest about where you are, so when you rewrite your story, you can have compassion for yourself, learn from the past, and move forward without feeling shackled to the person you once were. Don't create a future based on who you used to be.

Just Like Me

As we learned in the accountability chapter, forgiving yourself for regrettable past actions can be a powerful practice. When you begin to practice forgiveness toward yourself, you are then able to be more empathetic and compassionate for the journeys others are on. Below is a practice that I have adapted from a workshop I took years ago. All you have to do is put your attention on someone else. They don't even need to know you are looking at them—you could do this on the train, while taking a walk, or anywhere else you can create a bit of space to stand back and pause. Then, say to yourself:

- Just like me, this person has a story.
- Just like me, this person has experienced some kind of pain or suffering.

- Just like me, this person has experienced some kind of sadness, sorrow, or grief.
- Just like me, this person is learning about life.
- Just like me, this person is doing the best they can.
- Just like me, this person has struggled.
- Just like me, this person longs for a meaningful and fulfilling life.
- Just like me, this person is learning to compost their story.
- Just like me... you can fill in the blank.

What happens when you place your attention on someone else? What feeling is created for you? For me, I start to realize that we are all in this life together. I remember that we are all doing the best we can with our stories, perspectives, and beliefs. With this in mind, a feeling of compassion for myself comes over me. What's more, I also can have more compassion and empathy for others who are on their own journey.

The Practice of Shifting Perspectives

Though you cannot change a situation from your past, you can learn how to shift your perspective on it—to see it from a different angle. Our wounds can be our greatest gifts, and by shifting our perspective on them we can step forward to create a life of authenticity, purpose, and passion. Learning how to shift the way you look at a circumstance can change the way you look at life. For instance, if you believe that most everyone has ulterior motives and is out to get you, you might start to see through that lens regularly, and seek out moments that provide ample data that support your belief. If you are willing to shift your perspective and try on another belief, such as that people can act in ways that are less than ideal and also step into altruistic actions, kindness, and care, you begin to collect data on that idea, and in fact, you will begin to see more of these life-giving qualities in others.

The lens you choose to see the world through does not change the events that have happened in the past or the reality of what is going on in the world today. Instead, shifting perspectives helps you shift where you place your attention, which changes your experience of the world. Seeing the world as a beautiful place, for example, does not take away from the truth that there is still more work for all of us to do. Having the belief that the world is a beautiful place might change your energetic flow and lead you to the right people who can help solve the world's challenges.

When we have the courage to engage with our stories, we put ourselves into experiments to shift our perspective and are invited to see again with fresh eyes. Practicing shifting perspectives can lead you to feeling like you have renewed power—you are choosing how you want to view a situation, circumstance, or feeling. This is the first step to challenging the beliefs that don't serve us so that we can come home to what lives underneath the surface and compost that which seemed like our truth, but was in fact a well-etched groove. From that place we can begin to live out this new narrative, this new truth, our own truth, which often will feel more easeful, resonant, and life-giving.

ONE DEGREE SHIFT INQUIRY:
Challenging Your Beliefs

Usually when you feel like you are caught in the riptide of your life, there is a belief that is attached to it. So now it is time to start challenging these beliefs. Earlier, you wrote down some beliefs; now we are going to look at some of these same topics from the perspectives of your gremlin and your empowered self.

Sometimes (maybe even most times) when you shift perspectives, you need to practice this shift again, and again, and again, until it overrides the old groove. Your gremlins may want to resist you when you begin the process of shifting your perspective—this is where you can tap into your dedication and commit to a consistent practice. By doing so, you allow your new perspective and new way of relating to your old circumstance to take root and provide a new way of seeing, being, and consequently acting.

Write down your perspective from your gremlin self on the following topics:

1. Your body
2. Your self-worth
3. Love
4. Relationships
5. Money

Write down your perspective from your empowered self:

1. Your body
2. Your self-worth
3. Love
4. Relationships
5. Money

Now, reflect on these questions:

- What had to change to shift perspectives?
- What did you learn?
- Were there any perspectives that were easier to shift than others?
- What would it be like to challenge yourself and call yourself forth to see all of them from your empowered self; what would that take?
- What would you need to let go of to make that happen?
- Where else in your life are you being called to challenge or shift a perspective?
- How would that impact your life?
- What becomes available if you shift perspective?
- What is possible now?

What If *This* Was Fun?

Think of a situation in your life that isn't going the way you want it to. What would it be like to look at it from a different perspective? One of my favorite perspectives to take on any challenging situation is, "What if this was fun?" Especially the moments that many label as mundane, like cleaning the toilet, working late, or standing on the bus or train. All are ripe opportunities to shift perspective. How would your experience change if when you cleaned your toilet you envisioned a chorus singing with full gusto a song dedicated just to you and your sparkling toilet bowl? Or if on the bus or train you envisioned everyone as little toddlers in their happiest moment of play? It is so easy to get bogged down with the mundane or serious, yet when we step back and choose to see something in a new light, what seemed stagnant or dry can come to life in an unexpected and joyous way.

Maybe There Is More to Your Story Than You Know

I once heard a story about a farmer who lost his beautiful horse during a storm. Heavy winds knocked over the stable fence, and the horse went running off into the woods. The next morning the neighbors gathered around to console the farmer for his loss: "How unfortunate that your horse has run away." The farmer responded calmly, "We shall see."

Later that day, the farmer's horse came running back out of the woods, with three wild horses behind it. Again, the neighbors gathered and exclaimed, "Now you have your horse back and three new beautiful horses as well, how lucky!" The farmer said, "We shall see."

The next day, while the farmer's son was trying to tame one of the wild horses, he was kicked off the horse and broke his arm and his leg. The neighbors heard the boy yell painfully and came around

206 · One Degree Revolution

to see what had happened. "Oh no," they said, "now that your son has a broken arm and leg, who will help you with the farm? This is certainly an unfortunate circumstance." The farmer said, "We shall see."

The very next day, two soldiers came to the farm looking to recruit young men for the army, because the country would soon be going to war. They took one look at the farmer's son, who was severely injured, and said, "We cannot use this boy in combat; he may stay here at the farm." The neighbors caught wind of this news and ran over to the farmer to offer their excitement for the turn of events. "Now your son doesn't have to go to war and can stay on the farm with you, how fortunate you both are!" Once again, the farmer responded, "We shall see."

The lesson here is not to be detached from the events of your life. Instead, it's to be open to the mystery and possibility of what is waiting around the corner: that you can shift your perspective because you might not really see all of the parts of your story right now, in this moment. If you dwell on, are getting frustrated by, or are dissatisfied about a certain circumstance in your life, try to recall a situation or time that may have initially seemed negative or challenging, and that eventually evolved into a pleasurable or insightful experience.

Can you notice how that hardship or challenge created the space for a new experience to blossom? Can you stay open to the possibility that whatever situation you are dealing with now is simply the beginning of something bigger? As you look back at your story and see all the twists and turns of fate, does it seem to follow a logical and linear pattern, or is there a certain degree of mystery, surprise and, at times, unexpected coincidence?

The Sanskrit word *rahasya* teaches us another quality of consciousness: to trust that there are always things that are concealed, and that there is always more to be revealed. It teaches to consciously look at the world as if you are aware of only 25 percent of what's going on at any point in time, while there's another 75 percent that's concealed. If you then went on to learn another 25 percent, would you know half of everything? Rahasya teaches that you wouldn't: even when you learn and are exposed to more truths and experiences, there is even more that is hidden. Think about the universe and its vastness. We now know that our planet is the size of a grain of sand relative to the myriad solar systems, and there is so much more out there in space to be discovered. In this way, we can never know everything; there's always more to be revealed. There is always more in life to come.

Revealing what is concealed to us makes life interesting. We get to engage with the big-picture contemplations, and participate and change our perspective. Life becomes more joyful when we don't always know how the story ends because part of the process of uncovering can be a feeling of liberation. It's like the rocks and shells on the ocean floor that get concealed and then revealed when the tides go in and out.

The idea of seeking ultimate clarity in life has limitations (if it's even possible), because knowing how your life is going to unfold is like playing a game and knowing that you're going to win every single time. When I discovered rahasya it was a huge relief—once I let go of the desire or need to know everything, it allowed me to relax and appreciate where I was rather than where I was going. I could embrace the joy of remembering and forgetting and appreciate that this is part of the process of living.

Often, people will defend a perspective that actually keeps them stuck, putting themselves into a box of beliefs and saying things like, "Well, this is just how I am," or "This is just how life goes." While that may have been true in your past, you can always create a break in the narrative of who you think you are and how you think life works. Rahasya allows us to create space for a plot twist, which is exactly what you may need to make your life feel more whole and complete.

Rahasya also influences the way we look at our past. Have you ever had an experience that you thought was tragic and awful, yet when you look back on it you see how it actually was one of the best things that ever happened? When I was injured in my twenties and had the nine consecutive surgeries and was confined to my bed, I experienced a lot of sadness and frustration. It was challenging, but when I look back now, I can see that my time of quiet contemplation was one of the best gifts that I was given as a young adult, because it allowed me to create the gateway into having a deeper, more intimate relationship with life.

Though it wasn't immediate, shifting my perspective led me to see with fresh eyes. Being able to tap into my authentic self and realize that I was so much more than what my physical body could do led me to the power of living yoga. And what was concealed to me at that time was that so much of my life going forward was going to be centered around this practice of living yoga.

You can use rahasya as a way to check in when you are feeling out of alignment. To me, challenging your beliefs is a powerful one degree shift you can put yourself in. The truth is, we never know our whole story, so why not be open to the mystery of what may come, and participate in creating the next chapter, instead of getting stuck on what isn't working out for you. And most important, once you understand that we don't know everything, and that there is part of life that is concealed to us, maybe, just maybe, we can begin to challenge beliefs that don't serve us—maybe they are not as true as we once believed.

ONE DEGREE SHIFT INQUIRY:
Letting Go of the Life You Thought You Would Have

Too often we recycle our past hurts, drag them into our present, and let them inform our future. When we're stuck like this, we can throw away our hopes of what can be. Or sometimes, what can make you feel stuck is holding on to a life you thought you were going to have, or the idea of how you thought your life was going to go.

Be willing to let go of the life you thought you were going to have in order to let what is concealed come to fruition.

- Journal about the life you thought you were going to have. What "dream life" do you need to let go of so you can step into what is, rather than what isn't?
- Create some kind of ritual to let it go—it could be burning the pages of what you just wrote, or some way that could represent a change in perspective, and putting that life that you thought was going to be and those old ideas to rest. Make space for what wants to be revealed: the next chapter of your life!

Yoga Is Composting

I like to compare yoga to composting: we learn how to take the shit in our lives and turn it into something useful. It is the ultimate recycling project and a lesson in shifting your perspective on your stories so that you can compost them into the fuel to lead you toward the life you want to have.

When you are composting, you acknowledge that the story that created the dams and impressions does not change or go away. If you were abused or abandoned as a child, that is part of your truth. You can't change the fact that you lost your job. You can't change how you felt after your first romance ended. Of course there's a time to grieve, a time to be sad, a time when your story needs to be processed. The key is that your relationship to the story can shift, and that's how you get to be the victor rather than the victim of your historical narrative.

No story has a specific lesson attached to it. In fact, you decide what meaning you want to give your old story. So even when supposed "bad" things happen, the opportunity is to figure out how to compost this event into fuel for rewriting a more useful, more productive story. You have the opportunity to change the meaning of these stories, and you get to choose what meaning you want to make up about them. You get to turn the page, put your pen to paper, and write the next chapter, for the sake of seeing life more clearly, for participating in your personal evolution, freedom, truth, or whatever is next for you.

For instance, Emily, one of my students, was abused as a child. Being abused led her to create a belief that love means keeping a secret. This belief distorted her ability to see what was true and real, and created false narratives on what love looks like and feels like. This led her to unhealthy relationships, where she often chose to get involved with married men who told her that she was special and that she had to keep their relationship a secret.

Emily and I worked together to compost her story and make a major shift. We began by using the exercise below to look at how her old hurts were affecting her relationship choices, and then how composting those hurts could fuel a different story. Her story now still includes the past, but she doesn't allow it to frame the present. Her new story is: "I deserve love that gets to be known. I no longer have to be the secret." Today, Emily participates in her life with more awareness, and she is able to make different, life-affirming decisions. Before she gets into a new relationship, she pauses and checks in with herself and asks, "Am I just responding to that old story or do I get to say, 'Actually, I deserve a healthy, loving relationship where I am able to be appreciated, respected, and known'?"

ONE DEGREE SHIFT INQUIRY:
Composting the Old Story into a New Story

Here is a way of trying on new beliefs. If this exercise proves challenging, it might be because your gremlin has taken over, so remember that you have the ability to hold a boundary. It takes resiliency and effort to challenge beliefs that could be old and ingrained. Yet there is another possibility living on the other side of this dedication: a new truth, a new way to engage with the world, a new story that honors you in your brilliance.

1) Think of one aspect of your life where are you stuck—for example, money.
2) What is the current belief or perspective you hold about this area of your life?

   a) For example, the belief you might have is, "Money doesn't come easily," or "I'll never make enough money."

3) Ask yourself, "Am I willing to challenge this belief for the sake of a greater truth?"

a) If yes, keeping going to question 4.

b) If no, ask yourself if it's your gremlin speaking. Ask yourself, "Am I willing to try on a new belief?" You don't need
to know what to replace your old belief with yet. We're
just trying them on, like you would try on an outfit before buying it. The practice is to first create a boundary
with your gremlin so you have the space to try on the
new belief. You might imagine creating a line in the sand
that the gremlin can't cross—or letting the gremlin know
that it can come out later (if you want), just not now!

4) What are different beliefs that you could try on?

a) What would your empowered self say about your ability
to make money?

b) What would someone you love or respect have to say
about your ability to make money?

c) What does someone who came from poverty, then created financial abundance, have to say about your ability
to make money?

d) If you believe in a higher spirit or God, what would they
say?

5) What other perspective could you try on?

a) Money and abundance can come easily.

b) I believe in my ability to make money.

c) I am resourceful and will find ways to make money.

d) Creating money and abundance is a joyful adventure and
I can enjoy the ride.

e) I trust the unfolding of my life.

6) Pick the belief or perspective you want to live into as your truth. Don't worry about how to do it yet. Let go of being "realistic" and choose the one that best resonates with the life you want to live.

   a) For example, "I want to believe that creating money and abundance is a joyful adventure and I can enjoy the ride."

7) Once you have decided what belief you want—try it on! If this belief could come true how would this feel? What would be possible if you lived into this new belief? What would shift?

8) In order to live into this new belief, you need to brainstorm *how* you would need to shift.

   a) Create a boundary with the gremlin.
   b) Create a mantra around the new belief: "Creating money and abundance is a joyful adventure and I can enjoy the ride."
   c) Make a list of all the things you could say "yes" to in order to make this new belief a reality: For example, "I say yes to . . . resourcefulness, my resiliency, asking for help, creating a boundary with my gremlin, being responsible with how I spend my money, trusting the process, figuring out ways to save money, finding someone to help me make a budget."
   d) Make a list of all the things you need to say "no" to in order to make this new belief a reality. For example, "I say no to my gremlin, to spending more money than I have or living above my means, complaining about how to make

money, going out to lunch instead of bringing food from home, and buying coffee every single day."

9) Claim this new belief and try it on for the next seven days as your new truth. Start each day:

   a) Mantra from above (step 8b).
   b) Review your yes/no list from above (step 8c).
   c) Enroll your *kula*, or community, for support.
   d) Journal at the end of each day: write down what you are learning.
   e) At the end of seven days, either keep working with this new belief or try on another belief and go through the same process.

Changing the Cultural Perspectives

If you are stuck in old patterns of thinking, or believing that your way is the only way, can you try to look at an issue or circumstance from a different point of view? Shifting perspectives can also mean discovering new ways to look at the world, or brainstorming new ideas: both allow for more possibilities.

We have the power to take off our distorted glasses, as well as to challenge the beliefs that have been passed down generation after generation. By doing so, we can transform the cultural norms we blindly follow.

Changing a cultural norm can begin with the courage

to challenge a less than ideal belief or perspective. For instance, in the 1950s, the status quo for women was to stay home to cook and clean and raise their children. It wasn't until the 1970s when women began to challenge this way of thinking, proving that this model wasn't the only way to be in the world. They created the Women's Liberation Movement and a new reality started to emerge: it became acceptable for women to enter the workplace and be treated as equals to men. Though there is still more work to be done—women are still only paid 87 cents for every dollar that men earn—the cultural perspective for women has shifted. How can you be part of the cultural narrative shifting?

Rewrite Your Story

Now that you have challenged some of your long-held beliefs, you can begin to rewrite your story. You get to co-create your vision and write the next chapter, or what I like to call "Chapter 6/Chapter 7." Chapter 6 is your life up until this point. Chapter 7 could be a day, a week, a month, a year from now. It represents the possibility of your future narrative. Know that we don't need to plan out the entire book of our life; most of the time we only need to see ten feet ahead. By beginning to work on this vision of hope, things will start to shift. It's like a small batch of snow that begins to roll downhill and then, with the right elements, grows and snowballs into a powerful force. Focus on the small and from there allow this chapter to grow and influence the rest of your book.

ONE DEGREE SHIFT INQUIRY:
Chapter 6/Chapter 7

Write out chapter 6 as if your empowered self were writing. With fresh eyes, write down:

- What memorable events happened in your life up until this point?
- What fears or challenges did you face?
- What did you learn?
- Who were your allies on this journey, who offered support?
- What was concealed from you at the time?

Then start writing chapter 7, also from your empowered self—as if it has already happened!

Get creative, get specific—when you are a co-creator of your life, you can be optimistic. You can choose which perspective you want to look at your life through—you can decide what beliefs are useful! Take as much time as you want to write. Write about the dreams you accomplished, the freedom you felt, the courage you employed, the love you found, the abundance you opened to, the connections you made, the experiences you had, and the new beliefs you lived into! Allow yourself to live into possibilities!

You might consider some of these prompts as you write your next chapter 7:

- And then...
- What I evolved into...
- This dream came true by...
- I experienced...and it taught me...
- I discovered freedom by...
- I learned that true abundance is...
- I feel empowered now because...
- I know that I am worthy because...
- I now believe this about myself...
- What is possible now is...

Notice how it feels. Can you let yourself live in a world of possibility and hope? What had to happen to make that possible? Feel free to review all of the previous exercises in this chapter to support this process of writing your new story.

Create a Ritual

Now that you have begun rewriting your story, a daily ritual can help you embody it fully and create space for this new chapter to unfold. Creating a ritual can keep you on your path, compost your hurts into fuel, and participate in the next chapter of your life. A ritual can also take you out of the story that keeps you stuck.

You may decide to take time each morning for meditation, and for the next week, month, or year, dedicate your practice to whatever new beliefs and new story you want to live into: your chapter 7. You may want to say your new beliefs as mantras. You may decide to move your body in a way that embodies this new chapter and new beliefs—you don't need to study yoga postures to know what to do. For example, if you decide that one of your new beliefs is that you are powerful, think about how you would need to stand to embody power. If you are stepping into softness, what shape or form would your body move into? You may decide to include journaling in your ritual, or create an entirely different morning routine to help you put on the lenses you want to see life through each day.

Leave Room for the Unexpected

Even with our best intentions, life doesn't always go as we expect or plan. We are invited into life's twists and turns, and to honor the parts of life that are still concealed to us. Every moment of every day we have the opportunity to view our circumstances through whatever lens we choose. With enough practice, you start to realize how beautiful all the highs and lows of life really are—the texture they add to your existence.

You may need to tend to the aches in your heart, or your wounds, and there will be times when your old story and old beliefs may creep back in. However, I can promise that by doing the work, you will start to realize you are so much more than what happened in your past. You will start to realize you are part of this great mystery of life, and that there is more to it than any of us can ever completely see. When we can use our story as fuel for writing the next chapter of our life, when we remember there is always more to come, we can be more tender with ourselves and realize our wounds, stories, and hurts can be a portal into discovering what is true and real . . . and maybe we too can begin to see the magic that lives beyond the illusions that are holding us back.

The power lives within my hands.
Within this very breath and every breath,
I am invited to see life beyond fear, beyond fantasies,
beyond distortions,
and into that which is true and real.

Trust Life

I learned to trust holding on when it's time to hold.
To trust letting go when it's time to let go.
To trust what I know,
to trust what I don't know,
and to trust that everything is already okay.

Sometimes it can feel like life is more complicated than we can manage, with so many schedules or moving parts that need to fit together, or a host of different people to take into consideration. Other times life can seem like it is literally falling apart. This feeling of unraveling can lead to a sense of despair, especially when we focus on the painful events that are going on in our life, or even the world.

A typical response is to try to triage our lives, manage and prioritize everything around us even if we know that we are trying to control the uncontrollable. This intrinsic desire for control is understandable, and it has the tendency to provide us with only a false sense of security. The truth is, we can't control the future, and we can't predict exactly what is going to come our way. You could be hit by a car tomorrow, or realize a painting you bought at a yard sale is worth thousands of dollars, or that you have a sibling you never knew about! And, as much as we would like to, we also can't control other people's thoughts, actions, or behaviors, even if this desire is arising from an attempt to keep them safe or from making what we believe is a dire mistake.

Remember *rahasya*, which teaches that there are parts of life that are secreted or concealed from us, that our lives are constantly unfolding, and that we only really know what is right in front of us at any given time—and even that can be distorted! If you buy into rahasya, then how do you skillfully ride the waves when the unpredictable happens? The tools we've collected so far hopefully can help. The more you throw yourself into your own experiments and collect your own data, the more easily you can let go of the idea that life is supposed to go some particular way. By sitting in the fire and facing your gremlins; responding more often as your authentic self; becoming more accountable for your actions while practicing being comfortable with the uncomfortable; leaning in to your community; relishing in the power of pausing; taking time to reflect; and learning to compost old beliefs and beginning to rewrite your story, you might feel a greater sense of empowerment knowing that these tools better equip you to ride the waves no matter at what strength and height they come in. You can focus on what you can do, and let go of what you can't. When you learn to let go of the need to always control, you can make space—you create a fertile void for something else to begin to emerge.

By letting go of the myriad of things and ideas you can't control, you put yourself in a whole new inquiry, which I call "trusting life." The healthiest relationship you can have with life is committing to do the best that you can, and life is going to do what life is going to do. When you can accept this relationship, you can be more at ease with the unfolding of your own life, your own particular path, and the unfolding of the world around us.

ONE DEGREE SHIFT INQUIRY:
Exploring Letting Go

- What does trusting life look like?
- What would trusting life feel like?
- What could your empowered self say to your gremlin in order to let go and trust life?
- What would shift for you if you could start to let go of the uncontrollable? What becomes possible?

Life Always Wants to Thrive

Life is an ever-changing process, one that is flourishing and continuously blossoming. No matter how hard we try, life perseveres. Think about an asphalt driveway. Even though we intentionally pave over the dirt in front of our home, as soon as there is a crack, life takes it to be a window of opportunity. The next thing you notice is a weed, or blade of grass, pushing through. Instead of thinking of it as a nuisance, imagine that weed is saying, "I want to make it; there's more that I want to experience."

We are all made of this same life force that wants to thrive, and we have deep within us the desire to find the space to keep going in expressing ourselves—all we need is to find the crack in the driveway. Even in the worst conditions possible, there is a current moving through us. When we tap into that current, we can keep going and keep growing.

The one degree shift inquiries you have been putting yourself in are intended to show you different ways that your life might move forward, flow, unfold, blossom, and evolve. There is no "one way" or "right way" to do life, and in the moments when you feel uncertain which way to go, you can trust that ←THIS WAY→—either way, and *any* way—is still the *right* way.

Life Happens *and* I Get to Make Up the Reason

It's hard to trust life when it doesn't seem to be going the way we want. When this happens, we can make up great excuses for why we are stuck in the riptide. Or, when something happens that we wished hadn't, we can feel like the world is out to get us. Yoga teaches that while our actions largely contribute to how our life unfolds, at the same exact time there is the reality that some of the events of our life aren't as personal as we think. Sometimes, things happen for no reason at all.

This dichotomy is embodied in the yogic relationship of *karma* and *lila*. Like many Sanskrit words, karma has multiple definitions that aren't necessarily related. It's like the word "bark," which could refer to the outside of a tree or the sound a dog makes. In karma's case, in this context it means causality or consequence: if "x" happens, we'll most likely get "y." That's different than the karma yoga we talked about in chapter 1, which refers to the idea of selfless service.

Think about how many times you have heard that karma means "What goes around comes around," "everything happens for a reason"; or, when something bad happens, you may think of karma, and think, "Of course that would happen to me."

Karma teaches that there are consequences to our choices and our actions in that concentrated effort and dedication increase or decrease the probability of something happening. Yet at the same time, this concept invites us into a paradox: if life is always changing, then there is no such thing as certainty. In reality, karma only suggests that there is a high probability that something may occur; there is no guarantee. So if you smoke cigarettes every day, then there's an increased chance you'll get lung cancer. If you eat five to seven servings of vegetables every day, then most likely you'll reduce your risk for many diseases. If you drive through a stop sign every day, then most likely you'll get into an accident.

Lila teaches that sometimes things happen for no reason at all. Unlike karma, even though life is flowing in one direction, where it will take us is always a mystery. Lila reminds us that we don't know everything; we can't predict the future, so we can't always know why things happen.

Yoga teaches that karma and lila are always woven together. When our lives take a particular left turn, we will never know if it was due to karma or lila. Yet if we are open to the idea that they are both forces happening at the same time, we can learn to take the movements of life less personally. We can be in awe and wonder in the ways in which life works. This attitude can help us to be more comfortable being in the mystery, doing the best that we can navigating life's ups and downs.

I find karma and lila to be particularly empowering, and they are the reason that I don't buy into the expression "everything happens for a reason." Instead, I like to think of the comings and goings of life more as, "Things happen. Period. And I get to make up the reason."

When I experienced the nine knee surgeries in my twenties, there were plenty of people who told me that there was a proverbial pot of gold at the end of some rainbow I just couldn't see. They would say, "Oh, Coby, this happened for a reason. There's something that you're supposed to learn. Life is trying to teach you to slow down."

At first, these statements were confusing because as far as I could tell, the reality was that I just got injured, and there was no inherent meaning in the accident. Yet, it still presented an opportunity for me to make meaning out of it. For one, I had plenty of time to think about what I could do next and who I wanted to be. There were lots of lessons that I could get from the experience, and for me there was no bigger reason *why* it happened. It simply happened.

In the end, I could I trust that life isn't mean or retaliatory. We have experiences, and we're not being wronged for something we have done. We can trust that we can make up meaning that supports the person we want to blossom into.

My aim now is to create meaning around the events in my life that uplift and inspire me to be fully engaged, to be of service in some capacity, and to be a source of inspiration for others to do the same. So when things happen that aren't exactly what I expected, I can make up a meaning that provides the fuel for me to become a healthier version of myself.

ONE DEGREE SHIFT INQUIRY:
Living with Karma and Lila

When we can see the value of both karma and lila, we are invited to look more deeply at our life and make our best guess of what is needed.

- Describe a time when karma has played out in your life.
- What else becomes possible when you lean in to the idea of karma?
- Describe an experience when lila, or randomness, has played out in your life.
- What else becomes possible when you lean into the idea of lila?

Trust the Intelligence of Life

The next quality of consciousness is the concept of *chit*. In many yoga teachings, chit is defined as the "mind." Chit is also interpreted as "a great intelligence that is woven into the fabric of all existence." Yoga teaches that all of life is made from the same ingredients—whether you believe it is tissues, bones, blood, organs, or stardust—chit is the intelligence that weaves itself through every facet of life.

You do not need to believe in a higher entity to appreciate this intelligence (but of course, you can). Chit is seen everywhere in nature. And if you believe you are nature, then this intelligence streams through you too. Chit is the hundreds of automatic bodily functions we experience every day as well as the way the solar system harmonizes with gravity to allow us to experience life on Earth. It is the daily sunrise and sunset; the way a flower "knows" how to seduce a bee to pollinate again; why birds fly north only to fly south again; the cycles of the moon; a woman's menstruation; your heart beating; whales migrating; or a monarch butterfly knowing exactly the right time to burst out of its chrysalis and stretch its wings.

Chit teaches that there is intelligence to life which is profound, magical, and awe inspiring. When we feel disconnected, it may be because we have forgotten that we are nature, and that nature has an intelligence that works on its own schedule. For example, if we get a small cut, chit is what allows the body to start healing—we don't need to teach our blood how to coagulate, it simply knows. Yet we have a tendency to interfere with this intelligence because we forget about this inherent wisdom or the existence of the natural timing of this process. So, we mess around with the cut, layering on too many lotions or scratching it over and over and then wondering, "Why isn't this healing?" Chit invites us to trust the process and intelligence of life so that we can pause, step back, and actually move forward with much more ease. Often all it requires is patience and acknowledging where we evolved from, and then healing will naturally come.

When we accept the intelligence of the natural world, we can start to see its rhythms, patterns, and cycles, and then we can better align our lives with its flow. Think for a moment about the seasons. If you watch a tree lose its leaves in autumn only to see it renew itself again in the spring, you are witnessing an intelligent cycle that happens for a reason and repeats on purpose. Trees don't resist this flow of change, and can survive and even thrive through each new phase of their existence.

Just like trees, we have our own rhythms and seasons. We are always somewhere in the cycle as we live our lives and navigate changes and shifts: spring can bring new beginnings; summer is often the time for abundance in life; autumn reminds us of the power of transformation—that we need to let go so that we can begin the process of renewal; and winter allows us to slow down and rest for the activity that will come again in the spring.

Unfortunately, we sometimes forget how to be with each of these seasons. We can feel dissatisfied or even suffer when we're in one phase of life and we want to be someplace else. When we don't trust the intelligence of nature, and lose faith that change is part of the process, we often hold on to the past. For instance, even though nature shows us that change is beautiful, many people don't think that becoming old is beautiful: they do not trust that they will be attractive as they age, and do whatever they can to stay in the summer of youth.

While there's nothing wrong with celebrating the past or daydreaming about the future, we have an opportunity to learn how to savor each experience while we are having it, because ultimately there's no guarantee that a particular future will come true. We can't stand in the way of a new season coming, but we can honor where we are now, and learn how to create the most supportive meanings and actions to set ourselves up for a higher probability of success and ease.

When I was in my early twenties I was eager to be further along in my career. I longed to be a master of understanding human potential. One of my teachers used to say, "You can't be a master of anything until you're a masterful apprentice." This saying reminded me that it was an important part of my journey to slow down and to appreciate where I was. It reminds me to marinate in my now instead of always striving to get somewhere else, to stay open to what is right here before my eyes, and to trust that more will reveal itself.

ONE DEGREE SHIFT INQUIRY:
Chit Happens

Chit invites us to trust the intelligence of whatever season of life we are in, and reminds us that we can trust our feelings within each season. We can be with the joy and excitement of one season and feel sadness or grief in another. At some point you might see the beauty in sadness, in grief—and that just like the foliage, there is beauty in letting go.

Review different aspects of your life, such as relationships, friendships, studies, career, health, spirituality, finances, or any other category you want to explore. As you go through this next inquiry you might see that you are navigating different seasons for different categories, which is why we so often feel like we are treading water in the ocean, with so many different waves to ride at the same time. Life is movement—and the aim of this book is for you to learn to ride the waves with greater ease, as opposed to trying to still the waters.

This one degree inquiry reminds us that we don't need to focus on realigning everything at once. We can look at the areas of our life that are asking for the most attention, and from there give one or two or more parts of ourselves more time and care to see if we can make some loving shifts.

Ask yourself:

• For each of these categories, which of the seasons are you in?

- How are you engaging with that season? Are you skill-fully engaging or are you wishing it away? What is the impact?
- What advice would your empowered self offer to en-gage with this season? What do you need to say to your gremlin so you can trust this season and ultimately trust life more?
- What is one small shift that can lead you to be in a sym-biotic relationship with that season?

Decoding Advice

Often, when we call on our *kula*, or community, for advice, we'll receive thoughts and opinions that are based on the season that the other person or people are in. For example, if you are in the autumn of a breakup or divorce that is causing you an immense heartache, and your best friend is in the spring of a new relationship, she might suggest that you get back out there and start dating right away for the sake of recognizing your worth and value. That's sweet advice, and it might not feel like the advice that best applies to and supports your desire to pause, feel, and recalibrate before deciding on your next step forward.

The practice is to acknowledge that everyone is in their own season, doing the best that they can, and some-times colored by the season they are currently traversing. At the end of the day no one can walk your path for you or know exactly what you need. Be open to others' thoughts and suggestions, and remember, it's simply an offering—it doesn't mean it's the one degree shift that will serve you best.

In this way, when you find yourself being asked for advice or support by someone in your life, take time to put yourself in their shoes, to imagine what season they are in, and what might be the most useful way to support them. Simple questions like, "Is there any way I can support you right now?" or "What do you need right now?" or "I am here to listen if you'd like" are some of the best and simplest ways to begin offering support.

Trust There's Always Enough

Shri, often referred to as abundance, is another quality of consciousness. Abundance is the feeling of having enough, or being enough. Adopting an attitude of abundance is one of the small shifts that can have a big impact, affecting your worldview as well as your day-to-day life, including the way you go about your work, your relationships, and identifying your dreams. Take love, for example. Abundance means that I can love myself as much as I want, I can love others as much as I want, I can receive as much love as I want, and that still doesn't take away from how much love is available to the rest of the world.

Sometimes, people don't trust life because they are looking at certain situations through a lens of perceived scarcity. They are often bumping against the feelings of "I need more. I need to do more. I don't have enough. I am not enough. There isn't enough."

If you believe that you don't have enough, you might start to collect data that supports this belief. This data can feed your gremlin instead of your empowered self, and you may find that you are feeling stuck, looking through the distorted lens, creating false truths, and creating a worldview around a belief that might not be true. For instance, if you have a worldview revolving around scarcity, you might feel that if you go on a date that doesn't work out, you will be alone forever.

Yet *shri* reminds us that there is always enough, and sometimes all it takes is looking around in a different place. While it may be true that your date didn't work out, there are plenty of other people you can try to meet in a wide variety of settings.

There's also a huge difference between abundance, wishful thinking, and the law of attraction. Abundance isn't a guarantee of prosperity, nor is it about creating a vision board and wishing, "I hope I'll get a million dollars." Instead, I believe that abundance is available when you are willing to do the work. As I tell my students, hope is not a strategy. I once heard someone say, "You don't hope for dinner; you make dinner." You can't just sit there and wait for abundance to show up, in the kitchen or elsewhere.

When you believe that you come from abundance, you become more generous, are able to appreciate other people's successes, and begin to feel a sense of enough-ness. When we steep ourselves in abundance we can feel more grounded, connected, creative, free, open, loving—and ultimately, experience the feeling of trust toward what is possible. And when you learn to become more thoughtful in the ways in which you engage with life, there's a higher probability that you'll be able to cultivate and appreciate a greater sense of well-rounded prosperity that infuses the many areas of your life path.

Blueberries, Sperm, and Stars

When you start seeing the bounty all around you, you can engage with it and live from a place of having more than enough. Nature shows us so many examples of abundance. There are endless numbers of stars in the night sky, and there are even more stars that are still concealed to us. A blueberry bush produces what, at times, can seem like an unending amount of berries; if you've ever been blueberry picking, you know that you can stay and pick from one bush forever, even if a few blueberries end up in your mouth for a sweet snack. And while we only need one sperm to make it to the egg for human life to begin, it has to swim upstream with the multitudes of other little guys to get the job done.

ONE DEGREE SHIFT INQUIRY:
Finding Abundance

Yoga is skillful action, not skillful wishing or hoping. Though these strategies can support skillful action, they aren't the secret that guarantees abundance. If hope were enough, the whole world would be fed right now.

This experiment is to find how you can more skillfully participate in tapping into abundance now:

• What is your relationship to abundance?
• Where else can you see abundance?

- Do you trust that you live in an abundant, giving, loving world? Or are you hanging on to data you've collected from your past that's not allowing you to tap into life's prosperity? What is the impact?
- What would shift for you if you saw your life through the lens of abundance?

The Three "E"s of Abundance

My friend Leia works in an entry-level position and is dissatisfied and disgruntled with the hours and her relationship with her boss. She feels like there's nowhere for her to grow in her role, and that her boss is never going to give her more responsibility or a raise. Just knowing this little bit of information, I could see that Leia has a few options in how to navigate her current situation. She could quit her job and look for another that pays more and provides more opportunity for growth—assuming she has enough money saved to be unemployed for a bit. Or, she could see where she could be open to a different kind of abundance in the job she currently has outside her main challenges. She might not find it in her salary, yet there might be a richness in the interactions she has with her coworkers on a daily basis that actually feeds her sense of well-being. She could also tap into the abundance within herself to recognize that she is enough and worthy. She could also have a conversation with her boss about what she is feeling, the various ways she can take on more responsibility, and the reason she feels more money would support her performance. In this action also lives a great opportunity to ensure she isn't navigating this situation from a distorted perspective. A conversation could provide more data of what her next options may be.

Leia could also look at her current situation through another interpretation of abundance from Douglas Brooks. He teaches that the way to tap into abundance mirrors the intelligence of the natural world and its billion-year track record of continually thriving: taking actions that produce desirable results. And the best way to do this is what Douglas refers to as the three "E"s: efficacy, economy, and exigency.

Efficacy is how we measure the effectiveness of our actions. It is our ability to produce recognizable, conclusive, and desired results through the choices we make. A short walk in nature can help relieve a low mood. Avoiding coffee late in the day can make for a better night's sleep. Some cause-and-effect relationships will support you for a lifetime, while others might only be employed for a shorter time frame, depending on what you are trying to accomplish.

Understanding efficacy is the reason why living a life of inquiry is so vital; the more experiments you run, the more data you can collect to see what is working for you, and which behaviors need to be revamped. The key is to question why you choose to repeat a particular action or behavior if it is not yielding a desired result. People often think that working hard is enough to produce their desirable result (completing a marathon, finishing a project, raising a family, etc.), but who cares if you're working hard if it's not working? For Leia, she needed to figure out if she could get her desirable result—a pay increase—by explaining her situation to her boss. Leia could check in and evaluate if she was being clear; was she using effective communication to get her point across in regard to her value, her needs, and her contributions to the company?

Economy relates to thriftiness: using only the minimal amount of resources and energy we need to complete a task. We can look to nature to see this, where life chooses the easiest path for its own benefit, conserving both resources and energy expenditure. When water floods a canyon, it moves through the space by creating a pathway with the least amount of resistance. Economy encourages us to consider how we can achieve a desired result by putting in the right amount of effort. It asks you to consider the way you have structured your day, your relationships, and your work. It teaches that you don't need to meditate four hours a day; actually, ten minutes might be enough depending on what season you are in or what you are working toward. Why would you give 110 percent of your effort to complete a project and deplete yourself, when 100 percent would be enough? In Leia's case there was value for her to ask herself if the way she was working was economical, and if it wasn't, was that one of the reasons she felt she was underpaid for the long hours she was putting in at the office?

On the other hand, economy doesn't mean doing something half-heartedly. Why put in 95 percent effort and miss the mark? Economy teaches us that we would benefit from giving that last little bit of effort in order to generate more desirable results.

Exigency is the ability to take inventory of your limitations, and find ways to produce a positive outcome by being more resourceful. This is how we unlock our inner MacGyver. In nature, we can see exigency all around, whether it is birds gathering twigs, leaves, and feathers to construct a nest, or beavers carrying timber, mud, and stones to construct a dam. It is similar in our lives: often what we need to accomplish a task with more ease is right before our eyes, or close by. But because we have our blinders on and only look in one direction, we continue to walk forward dragging through the mud, when in fact that which would enhance our resourcefulness is so near.

Leia could get creative about ways in which she could be more resourceful, and find ways that would make her current job more manageable. For instance, while there might not be more money in the budget to get a raise, what if she was able to negotiate working from home one day a week? This would encourage her to be more economical throughout her week, save money on one fewer day of childcare, and have more money to spend on her self-care, which would hopefully support her in being more energized and fulfilled with her job.

Leia realized that when she tapped into the abundance of what was already available to her, she could appreciate her current job a bit more. She also became more efficacious, and expressed her feelings to her boss. Together, they were able to evaluate her workload and see how she could work more economically. They realized that if she worked from home two days a week, she could save money on daycare for her kids. Then, they crafted a new, more resourceful schedule that worked for everyone. Leia now feels more positive about her job, and realized that abundance was actually right there before her.

ONE DEGREE SHIFT INQUIRY:
Exploring the Three "E"s

Efficacy:
- Where are you continuing an action that is not producing a desirable result?
- What is an inquiry you could put yourself in to make a shift?

Economy:
- Where are you doing too much or too little—what is the impact?
- What is a small shift that you could make to show up at 100 percent?

Exigency:

- Where could you be more resourceful? Where in your life can you make something out of nothing?
- What is one small shift you could make to get inventive? How could you tap into abundance to obtain what you need?

Trust the Mystery

Another way we can learn to trust life is by letting go of the idea that we should know all the intricacies of how life is supposed to work, or that every aspect of life is always going to make sense. Even if you think you have your finger on the pulse of politics, raising children, or your own story, *rahasya* teaches us once again that there is always something that's being secreted, and there will always be more for you to learn. There's always the possibility that you have come to the wrong conclusion. As I like to say, leave room for doubt.

Just because I'm not going to know everything doesn't mean I'm not interested in diving into the inquiry of the mystery of life, of the not knowing. To me that's still a fascinating idea that actually adds to the sweetness and enjoyment of life, rather than creating disappointment or frustration. I'm excited that there are always more questions, there are always more inquiries, there are always more adventures into the unknown.

It's difficult to let go of the idea that everything should make sense and all of our inquiries and questions about life can be answered. Think about it this way: when we can let that need to know everything go, we actually can get more curious about what we don't understand. And if you are not ever going to know everything, the next experiment can be to figure out what else you are interested in exploring.

For instance, my mother once had an experience that goes right to the heart of the mystery of life. She was very close with her parents, and when she was in her thirties, her mother suddenly died. My mother was beyond heartbroken. Though she did not grow up with any particular faith, she wanted desperately to know what happened when we die, and if her parents would ever be reunited. So she and my grandfather made up a password that only they knew. The plan was that when my grandfather died, if he was with my grandmother, somehow the password would be delivered to my mom. She never told anyone the password, but she did share with me that she had made this pact.

As the years went on and my grandfather was reaching the end of his life, my mother would remind him, "You remember the password, right?" When he passed away, I immediately called my mother, wanting to know if I could support her in any way. And in my curiosity, I asked if she had heard the password. All of a sudden she got really quiet, and I could tell she was holding back tears, and finally she said yes.

The password was not a common word that you might expect to hear in everyday conversation—like "beautiful," or "sunshine," or "love"—it was "go-kart," and she heard those exact words just a few hours after my grandfather passed away. They chose that word because when my mom was little she had once made a go-kart with my grandfather, and when it was finished they wanted to take it for a test drive. My grandmother was adamantly against it. She cautioned them, "No! You are going to hurt my daughter in that thing!" But my grandfather took my mom out anyway, and within a few minutes she crashed. When they came back home my grandmother was so grateful that her baby girl was unharmed that under her breath she muttered, "Ugh, that damn go-kart." And from that day on, that phrase became an inside joke, a funny memory they all cherished. On the day my grandfather died, on the way to the funeral home, my mother was driving in the car with someone who didn't even know there was a password. A small car pulled up next to them and he said, "Looks like a damn go-kart," in the exact same tone that my grandmother used the day of the crash.

When I heard this story, it opened my mind to accepting that there would always be mysteries in life. That maybe, just maybe, I don't know everything that is going on. And in that not knowing lives infinite possibilities. And when I am open to the current of mystery, I'm filled with a feeling of hope, of wonder, and of trust.

ONE DEGREE SHIFT INQUIRY:
Where Is There Mystery?

- Can you think of a story in your life that can't be explained with logic or reason?
- What could shift if you allowed yourself to be open to the acceptance of mystery?

Surrender and Soften

Surrender is the feeling of taking off your shoes at the end of the day; a deep sigh of relief, an exhale that can lead to a softening from the inside out—you can finally let go of the tight grip and open into ease. The practice of surrendering reminds us that we can't, nor are we being asked to, do it all. Imagine squeezing your hand into a fist, and holding, holding, holding, holding, holding that position so tightly for so long that your fist becomes hardened as if it were encased in a cast. But once you let go and take the cast off, you can have greater range of motion, which actually allows you to experience more of life.

You are more likely to experience this feeling when you trust life, because once you let go of trying to control the uncontrollable, the need to know everything, and a worldview of scarcity, you've actually built a new roadmap for yourself. Then, when you find that you are feeling misaligned, you can trust that life is a journey of twists and turns, and is not a problem to be solved. You can have trust and faith that you can always put yourself into another experiment. While you may not have all the answers, you can do you and let life do the rest. That in and of itself can help you feel more at ease, even safer that ultimately everything is already okay. And when people feel safe, they're more likely to relax and surrender.

In yoga class, we like to say that when you let go, you can receive the benefits of your effort or your work. This can also be true off the mat, whether you are looking for healing, joy, openness, or creativity. When we surrender we can receive information and insight, and be open to whatever is trying to get our attention.

A lot of people make the beautiful choice to become social justice warriors so that they can make a real change in the world. Yet even when we are on the noblest crusade we need to take care of ourselves. Surrendering in this context means giving yourself a break. It's true that we can always do better or do more, and there are many issues that need to be addressed personally and globally, yet we can't take on the whole world and its problems all of the time. It's also okay to let go of the good fight when that particular season has passed and just enjoy your life, even when the world's problems aren't all tidy or solved.

In the next chapter, we're going to explore what calls to you, so you can feel empowered to take action rather than focus on what you can't do. And for now, what if part of the solution was actually taking time to refill your well by finding the simple pleasures of life, learning to trust life itself, and surrendering?

Give Us a Break

When we trust life and practice surrendering, it allows us to be gentler with others. Almost everyone is learning to ride the waves of life, learning how to be with their different seasons, and learning to trust life, too!

You are also invited to forgive yourself for your moments of misalignment and to give others a break.

• What becomes available when you give yourself space to "be human"?

• What shifts when you give others space to be human and to learn through the times they find themselves off course?

ONE DEGREE SHIFT INQUIRY:
Feel the Release

What does surrendering—the act of doing *not-doing*—feel like? Well, if you've ever taken an *asana* yoga class, you may be familiar with *savasana*, or corpse pose. Lots of yoga classes end this way, where you lie down with your hands and feet apart, and deeply exhale as you rest for a bit of time. Each time we practice savasana we are practicing the art of letting go, and for some people this is the hardest pose.

You can practice savasana right at home. Carve time out to lie down on your back, get comfortable, cover your eyes, play relaxing music, and put on a gentle timer for as long as you need. You can practice even for a minute, or as long as would feel nourishing.

Take a few deep breaths with expansive exhalations. Allow the breath to soften and recede into the background. Envision your body sinking into the support of the ground, soften, and let go. Give yourself permission to simply be and rest. When the gentle alarm rings, take several minutes to breathe, move your limbs, stretch, roll over to one side, notice how you feel, and return back to your day.

Surrendering Can Mean Choosing to Do Nothing

Part of trusting life is learning to find your center within the flow— to address any moment of unease by taking a breath, or aligning with your empowered self, or creating a boundary with your gremlin, or remembering there is power in asking for help, or understanding that sometimes life will get hot.

So far, the lessons in this book have been about skillful action, and putting yourself in new experiments. In short, there's been a lot of doing. And what if sometimes the most skillful way to participate, create change, or work with your gremlins is simply to do nothing? At some point, the most skillful action we can do is to not act, and to trust life to just hold us, and to be carried. Let the fruits of your labor hold you for a while. It's kind of like when you were little, you and your friends created a whirlpool by walking in the water, all in the same direction. After you worked hard to get the water flowing, you could float in the water and it would just carry you.

Surrendering can mean trusting that whichever way you go, you can always put yourself in another experiment. Sometimes the best thing to do is do nothing. And sometimes the best thing to do is to do something. So how do you know when to do nothing, and when to do something? Yoga is a path that provides zero answers but does provide infinite inquiries and experiments. Every time you put yourself into one, see if it produces a desirable result; if it doesn't, try something different until you are satisfied. And one of the options is always to do nothing and see where life takes you.

The one degree shifts throughout this book are ways to learn to flow with life with more ease. But the truth is, you are always in the flow of the river. Even when you get out of today's riptide, tomorrow you very well may be sucked in again. That's the rhythm of life, and where we can learn to trust that the waves will come, that rhythm and movement are not problems that need to be solved. It's not personal, it's just part of being human. And, as we get more proficient at recognizing the waves, we can respond to them more quickly and with greater ease.

When the leaf is ready to fall from the tree,
it falls.
Because it trusts the intelligence of life,
the rhythm of life.
It is time to let go
and trust the process.
Though this season is ending,

a new season is emerging,
yet unlike the leaves, we seem to go against nature.
We cling.
We grasp to what was and what we know.
But all we need to do is remember that the leaf is meant to fall,
to compost into the earth
and merge into winter,
for the rebirth of spring,
and flourish into summer,
simply for autumn to come again.

10

Callings

Knock, knock.
Your life is calling.

❧

"W hy am I here?" is one of the questions I hear most often
from my students who long for meaning and purpose in
their lives. What they are searching for seems to be true for the rest
of us: we know that happiness is more than having a steady career or
accumulating material possessions. We want our life to be fulfilling,
and we don't always know the right way to figure out how, or what's
actually missing.

As we discussed in chapter 1, yoga teaches that one of the four
aims of living a fulfilling life is to discover and claim your life's purpose, your *dharma*. I like to think of dharma as the essence of who you
want to be in the present moment, not just the job you want to have
or the kind of work you want to do. It is not a fixed or predetermined

destiny based on some particular talent. Life is a never-ending process, and your dharma may evolve.

Claiming your purpose allows you to create a tangible plan, and with that can come a sense of inner calm, a deep exhale of relief. A purpose can also provide a feeling of contributing to the world in a useful way, and to participating in something greater than yourself. So how do you start this dharma experiment? The truth is, most people are already swimming near their purpose: it's close by, maybe even part of your life already. You can consciously connect to your life purpose: sometimes it is an obvious and clear recognition that informs how you take your next steps. Other times it is a yearning that lives in the background that you are not even aware of, and somehow you are drawn toward it. What seems to be true in both instances is that there are usually signals trying to get your attention, and when you recognize and respond to these signals you start to feel more aligned with this idea as you edge closer to whatever it is that you want to be doing, living, or experimenting. I think about these signals as your *callings*. So let's turn up the volume and tune into what's trying to get your attention.

Big "C" and Little "c" Callings

A calling is a whisper trying to get you to shift something, do something, be something, or try something. It is the idea that keeps swirling around in your mind, or is knocking at your heart and wants your attention. Or, it could be the vision that would break your heart if you didn't do it, or the cries of the world you hear. A calling might wake you up in the middle of the night or is the energy that moves you to get out of bed in the morning. And, a calling doesn't have to be earth-shattering—there are plenty of small callings that also are trying to get your attention and are worthy of exploration.

Mother Teresa was called to help the less fortunate, Van Gogh was called to be an artist, and Amelia Earhart was called to adventure. We recognize that certain individuals were called to do certain things. If that's true of some people, could it be true of all of us?

A calling might be a woman listening to her inner urge to become a mother, a person who loves nature and chooses to spend more time in a garden, or someone who is dedicated to their health and enjoys cooking nourishing food. A calling could be to experience more passion or more peace, or to feel contentment. A calling could be to pay off your debt and find financial freedom. A calling could be to start meditating. A calling might be to heal your tender heart, or to learn about love. A calling could be to cut your hair, travel the world, or start a business. A calling could be something as simple as painting your living room a radically different color, or pursuing volunteer work that aims to end sex trafficking.

Each one degree shift inquiry is its own type of calling. If you participated in any of the inquiries in the book, whether it was to ask for help, pause, rewrite your story, etc., you were responding to a call; you chose which ones to participate in because you were called to them. In the process of seeing the inquiry through, you may have received new data and were able to make a small shift.

I believe that callings fall into two different categories: Big C (Big Calling) and Little c's (little callings). The Big C is your dharma, or life purpose. It begins to answer the question, "What is the essence of who I want to be and what am I here to do?" The little c's are all of the nudges that point you toward an action that can lead to making a change. These two types of callings can be in synchrony, working together to support your dharma or life purpose. For example, if your Big C was to support others, you might have decided to listen to little c's that guided you toward studying psychology or education to support your Big C. Or the little c's can support the other areas of life you might be exploring, or one of the other aims of yoga—*kama* (your desires), *artha* (inner and outer prosperity), and *moksha* (liberation and freedom), and may have nothing to do with your Big C life purpose at all.

You can use the inquiries in this book to help you identify your little c's and your Big C. And each of the lessons may serve you as a way to prepare for answering a calling. For instance, you might have to practice becoming comfortable being uncomfortable for the sake of your calling. The more you are aligned with your authentic self or living with integrity, the easier it will be to recognize your calling. You can also remember that you are never in the maze alone: you can always lean in to your community as you answer a calling. Meditation can provide the time and space to reflect on your calling. And there is value in the moments of pausing to savor the experience as you are going through it. You can check in and see if your beliefs and the next chapter of your life are aligned with your purpose, or if composting past hurts into new energy can be used to support your calling. And when you can trust life and the knocking that is trying to get your attention, you can surrender to the process and take comfort that your efforts are all part of this sacred journey called your life.

So what is trying to get your attention? Let's start to explore your Big C first, and then we can determine what little c's might need to be tended to, and how they may or may not be related or supportive to your Big C.

Discovering Your Dharma: The Big C

A Big C is your big calling, your life purpose or your dharma: it is like a compass that points toward your true north. Your Big C can begin to answer the question, "What values do you care enough about to actually bind yourself or yoke yourself to today?" Your Big C can feel like an absolute *yes*, and provide you with a stake in the ground so that you can take a firm stand for what you believe in.

When we talk about finding your Big C in my workshops, some worry that discovering their Big C is too big of a task to take on. Some find it difficult to stand in their own light, think that their life purpose seems too big an ask to claim. Yet the truth is, when we feel "off" it could be because we are not living in alignment with it. In some ways, not doing the work to claim your life purpose is a cop-out, because when you say "I don't know what my life purpose is, and I can't figure it out," you're avoiding the consequences of putting a stake in the ground. When you take a stance, you own what you believe in. You can imagine what impact you can have. For example, if you claim that your life purpose is about spreading kindness, your daily behaviors of actually spreading kindness will open you to seeing the ripple effect your actions have on those around you.

Too often people let their desire for absolute clarity of the "right" life purpose get in the way of doing the work. Others fear that claiming a single life purpose will make them feel stuck to a particular path that won't be a perfect fit. The truth is, we never know in advance if following any particular path will lead us to our most desired result; all we can do is put ourselves in the experiment. By doing so, we get to engage with a beautiful paradox of both staying committed to our actions, focused on our outcomes, and at the same time remaining open to the fact that sometimes even our best efforts don't turn out the way we intended. And when this happens, you always have the choice to put yourself in another experiment.

There is power in practicing just for the sake of practice, and part of the work is not to be overly attached to a particular outcome. The practice is to have a healthy attachment, and at the same time to let go of the tight grip of how it is all supposed to turn out—and remembering there is always more to come; something just might be concealed from you right now. If you take a step in a direction that doesn't seem to serve your deepest calling, it's okay. You have the opportunity to make another choice and step in a different direction. You can always begin again. In fact, it is guaranteed you will begin again, time after time. To walk the path of living your callings is to listen to your inner compass, to trust it, to lean into it, and to keep on walking.

Even if you find a purpose that later reveals itself not to be an exact match, it could be a one degree shift that can lead you closer to what you are seeking. As the *Bhagavad Gita*, a yogic text, suggests, it is better to live your life imperfectly than to try to live someone else life's perfectly. There is no single right way to live life; we are all doing the best we can. While so many people envision a linear trajectory for their personal and professional lives, what ends up happening looks much more like a zigzag. When you have the inner strength to stay committed to your path as it continues to be revealed, you will eventually see how it all fits together.

One experiment you can do to discover your Big C is to pay attention to what has heart and meaning for you. The answers will often relate to your values. It might be about creative expression, or healing, or spreading kindness and love—or it might be the voice of activism, fierce energy, or your passion for not accepting the status quo that stirs the pot. For instance, my dad, who's never practiced the downward-facing dog kind of yoga, is one of the most *yogic* people I've ever met. He would give the shirt off his back to anybody who was in need. To me, he's living his Big C by being kind and generous with his time and attention.

A Big C does not have to be as specific as we might think. Kindness or peace or compassion might just be enough. Imagine if we all lived our lives being loving, how different our world would be.

It can take courage to live your life purpose, to put yourself out there in a way that others might not value or think is best for you. Too often we are living a life that is based on other people's expectations and values, or a life that we once enjoyed, but have outgrown. So many people live without identifying their own values and end up feeling disconnected because they are trying to live by someone else's rules or vision, and it isn't working. Over time disengagement can brew greater doses of dissatisfaction because life is being lived solely from the outside in—trying to make everyone else happy, living a life *they* think you should live.

ONE DEGREE SHIFT INQUIRY:
Identifying Your Values

If you are curious as to what your values are, notice what you care about most, what you find yourself talking about to other people, or what qualities you admire about others who inspire you. What makes you want to be alive, and not just live? What are you interested in and curious about? For instance, if you are nourished by meaningful conversations with a friend, you most likely value connection. If you are passionate about taking care of the earth, one of your values may be respect. If you love skinny-dipping on a warm summer night, you might value a sense of freedom.

In the first column, list ten activities, interests, or passions that light you up and make you feel more alive. In the second column, write out the value that you think each correlates to. You might also notice that the same values show up several times, which is perfectly normal and will hopefully help you reach a greater understanding of what you value most in your life. Keep in mind that you may unveil many values, because we all have more than one.

What Makes You Feel Alive?	(Potential) Correlated Value
1.	
2.	
3.	
4.	
5.	
6.	
7.	
8.	
9.	
10.	

Here's how I would complete this exercise:

What Makes You Feel Alive?	(Potential) Correlated Value
Competing in triathlons	Like-minded community
Picking flowers	Appreciating beauty
Drinking green juice	Vitality
Ecstatic dance	Full expression
Walking in nature	State of awe
Streams and waterfalls	Appreciating beauty
Teaching	Sharing knowledge by bringing people together
Painting	Full expression
Hosting a party or gathering	Bringing people together
Trying something for the first time	Learning

For the Sake Of

When you claim your Big C, you need to get clear and committed as to *why* you are compelled to answer this calling. The way I like to refer to this reason is "for the sake of." It should express what you hope will be accomplished by following this calling, the stance you are willing to take that is related to it: your proverbial stake in the ground. Your Big C should feel so important that you are willing to sit in the fire of discomfort in order to live it.

Your "for the sake of" statement should be strong, so that if your gremlins try to take over, you will feel prepared to face and engage with them. For example, if you are called to spread truth, your "for the sake of" might be to live a more honest, sincere, and transparent life. Now, imagine if your gremlin shows up when your boss is telling you something that you know isn't true. The gremlin is whispering for you to keep quiet and not rock the boat. But because you have taken a stance on truth, you may feel more empowered to find a way to communicate your truth, stand up for yourself, and communicate in a clear and nonviolent way.

ONE DEGREE SHIFT INQUIRY:
Claiming Your Big C with a Life Purpose Statement

Let's go a little bit deeper and put these pieces together to create a life purpose statement, which will include your values and your "for the sake of." First, to find where you might already be putting a stake in the ground and uncover more of your values, read each prompt, and respond to it by writing down your thoughts as quickly as possible. Give yourself no more than three minutes for each one.

1. You are at a party, for you! Everyone you love and care about is attending this party to honor your life. Everyone will give a speech on how you have touched their life. What do they say? How do they feel about you? How would they describe your impact?
2. Imagine that you were given an opportunity to speak in front of the entire world. You are calm and excited, speaking from your heart. You are there to inspire and encourage. Your audience is waiting

with anticipation and attention. What would you say? What would your message be? What would everyone walk away feeling? What would be possible now?

3. You have been given a superpower: the ability to make people deeply connect to an emotion. You may use this power however you want. What would you want people to feel? How would you want to feel? Why did you choose this feeling? How would you describe this feeling—through color, image, metaphor, song, etc.?

4. You have a bumper sticker on your car that everyone who passes will read and be inspired by. What would it say? What effect would it have?

Review your answers, and compare them to the results of your values inquiry. Look for common themes or threads. Now, take these values and complete the sentence below: this will be your life purpose, Big C, dharma statement—at least for now. Read it a few times and feel if it resonates. You might feel an energy running through you when the statement is aligned to your inner compass. Don't overthink it; like my dad says, "You think long, you think wrong."

I claim today that my Big C is to _____ **for the sake of**_____.

Here are some real life purpose statements from some of my students:

- I claim today that my Big C is to be a student of life for the sake of curiosity, humility, and openness.
- I claim today that my Big C is to embody truth and heart for the sake of inspiring others to do the same and to create a more honest world.
- I claim today that my Big C is to be a beam of support and light for the sake of freedom.
- I claim today that my Big C is to gather people for the sake of shared responsibility so we can create a more compassionate world.

The Little c's

While your Big C is your essence, your little c's—notice that there are more than one—might point the way to making choices that support your values (although they do not have to). Your Big C could be an expressive force of creativity, and you might have a little c to go to art school. Your Big C could be to become a steward to Mother Earth, and you might have a little c to get a job working for an environmental group. If your Big C is to be an expression of generosity, your little c might steer you to send your friends care packages when it's not a birthday or holiday, or volunteer in a soup kitchen. If your life purpose is to support others to heal, a little c might include the desire to get healthier yourself.

Then, within each particular little c, there are more things you can do, and each will be its own little c. If one of your little c's is getting healthier, other little c's might come up, like eating fewer processed foods, starting to move your body in a more consistent way, or deciding to try a one degree shift by cutting out sugar, dairy, or gluten.

A little c could be to quit a job, pay off your debt, prioritize a healthy lifestyle, heal your relationship with family, write a book, go on a trip around the world, leave a dysfunctional relationship, or start a business, slow down, savor more, learn to relax and not take everything so seriously, or find your tribe. The list is infinite. Often our little c's serve as a nudge to get us back into alignment. They allow us to ask ourselves, "Where are we committing a crime against wisdom?"

Little c's can also be the aspects of life that impact your day-to-day existence: career, marriage, home life, who you hang out with, what you study in school; and they can add up to support the essence of who you are. This is why people often think that their little c is their Big C. Yet if you haven't explored what really fulfills you, and you assume you're supposed to want the commonly held goals of life, those little c's aren't going to be fully satisfying. That in itself might be the sign that shows you that little c's aren't enough to be your purpose.

However, just because they're little doesn't mean that little c's are always easy. Most would agree that a marriage takes effort, or that building a career can take time. And just like with the Big C, don't let your desire for absolute clarity get in the way of taking some kind of thoughtful action. Sometimes throwing yourself into the experiment is the little c that is calling you right now. And know that trust and faith says that if you say yes to a little c and you end up in a place that doesn't feel right, you simply listen again and act again, and trust that life is self-correcting.

Again, Beware the Gremlins!

It is almost guaranteed, and it's not bad or wrong, just simply true, that you might awaken the gremlins—the self-sabotaging parts of yourself—when you are called to anything that matters, like your Big C or important little c's. Answering your callings can offer the perfect opportunity for the gremlins to create disorder under the disguise of preserving your current reality and maintaining a false sense of safety. They might show up in the form of doubt and chime in to say, "Not now, not now, not now." Or, your gremlins will try to create apathy, fear, or inertia by whispering, "You shouldn't take that leap," or "You can't do it," or "You're not good enough," or "Be grateful for a nice life," or "Don't rock the boat."

Instead of giving up, we have the opportunity to be in relationship with these gremlins. Whatever you're being called for, you need to be committed to that calling above your own comfort because when the gremlins show up, they most likely will make it uncomfortable. You'll be invited to sit in the fire again, face the gremlins, and do the work in order to let your empowered self confidently face resistance, fears, and all the emotions that may arise.

When you say yes to your little c's you are participating in and co-creating your life. This can be the inspiration for other people to do the same, because when they see that you can do it, it can give them hope that they can too. When I was in my early twenties I had a little c to travel for a full year on my own, something I had never done before. At the time I was working as a district manager for a corporation. I decided to start making choices and one degree shifts that supported my little c. I needed to look at how I was going to save for this trip, so when I moved into a new apartment I kept the place mostly empty. All I bought was a bed and a few dishes. I cooked at home rather than eating out, and I made a commitment not to purchase anything that wasn't a necessity for living. All these shifts supported my little c to travel the world, and my friends saw the small shifts that I made and how I was able live this dream. They were able to think about the little c's that were calling them, and see that a small shift in how I prioritized my spending really led to living out a big dream.

All the while I was working at my job, doing the best I could, and planning to quit when I had saved enough money. As I got closer, I told my boss my plans and gave him plenty of time to fill the position. When my departure date for my world trip was near, the company gathered for a staff meeting and I was offered a promotion and a substantial raise! The practical part of my brain, which houses my gremlins, was loud and clear: "How can you turn down all that money? Put the trip on the back burner, you don't even speak another language." "How will you find your way around?" My boss (an outside gremlin voice) told me I would never get another opportunity like this again. I knew that my little c meant something to me, and it gave me the courage to stand my ground. I quit my job and began my travels. And though there were moments that my gremlins wanted to take over and make me doubt my decision, it ended up being one of the best little c's I have ever said yes to.

The Chakras and Little c's

You might be able to point quickly to some of your little c's because they are right there on the surface of your life. These are the small shifts you may have already identified through the exercises in this book, or the things on your to-do list. Yoga also offers teachings that can help, and one that I find particularly practical and useful is the *chakras*. The term "chakra" is derived from the Sanskrit word meaning "wheel" or "circle," and refers to energy centers that are correlated to different parts of the human body. A contemporary perspective views the chakras as a road map to access key life qualities like stability, sensuality, personal power, love, communication, intuition, and interconnectedness. When these centers are open and the energy flows easily through them, they can help us function better on a physical, emotional, mental, and spiritual level.

It is important to note that although these centers are represented individually, in reality the chakras are one system. So, if you are called to address one chakra, most likely you will feel the impact everywhere. Often people will talk about working with the chakras sequentially; however, I believe whichever one needs tending to is the one that is worthy to explore. Let go of what you may have heard about the chakras, and trust what is trying to get your attention.

You can use this simplified version of the chakras to look for potential little c's. For example, if you are just out of a relationship and feel like you've lost your sense of self, look at your third chakra, which supports reclaiming your personal power. If you feel like your whole life is pragmatic and in your head, you might be called to the chakra that invites you into your heart.

Muladhara: Foundation or Root

The first chakra resides at the base of the spine and influences physical stability, safety, grounding, and foundation. It is related to our survival instinct, the ability to remain centered, an experience of home, and the health of the physical body. This area of stability correlates to the element of earth.

When this wheel is balanced you might feel grounded, a sense of safety, or connection. When it is out of balance, you might experience disconnection, feeling unsafe, aloofness, anxiousness, panic, and an inability to take clear action.

ONE DEGREE SHIFT INQUIRY:
Finding Your Root

• Do you feel at home in yourself?
• Do you feel rooted and grounded?

If your answer to either of these questions is "no," then maybe your first chakra is calling you. What might be a one degree shift that you could put yourself in to feel more balanced? For example, you could spend more time in nature, eat foods that grow underground such as root vegetables, or practice yoga postures that are grounding, such as a yogic squat.

Svadhishthana: Fluidity

The second chakra resides about two inches below your navel and influences your emotional experience, sensuality, fluidity, creativity, openness, and sexuality. It is related to our ability to go with the flow, to stay adaptable and open. This area of fluidity correlates to the element of water.

When this chakra is in balance we might feel more open to receive, more creative, and passionate. When this wheel is out of balance you might experience an emotional disconnect, lack of creativity, fear of vulnerability, rigidity in thought, guilt, or an inability to adapt to change.

ONE DEGREE SHIFT INQUIRY:
Flowing with Life

• How open and fluid do you feel? Are you able to flow with the highs and lows of life?
• Do you feel connected to your creativity or gifts/talents/strengths?

If your answer to either of these questions is "no," your second chakra might be calling you. What might be a one degree shift that you could put yourself in to feel more balanced? For example, you might decide to try some artistic or creative project, spend time in water, or do circular pelvic movements.

Manipura: **Empowerment**

The third chakra resides in the solar plexus—or about three inches above your navel—and influences our power, vitality, self-esteem, and our ability to create healthy boundaries. It reminds us that we matter and that we can find our inner strength when we value what we share with the world. This area of empowerment correlates to the element of fire.

When this chakra is balanced we might feel confident, empowered, and assertive. When this wheel is out of balance we might experience low self-worth, passive-aggressive behavior, critical self-condemnation, or we might knowingly allow others to take advantage of us.

ONE DEGREE SHIFT INQUIRY:
Claiming Your Power

• Do you claim your self-worth?
• Do you create healthy boundaries?

If your answer to either of these questions is no, then maybe your third chakra is calling you. What might be a one degree shift that you could put yourself in to feel more balanced? For example, you might practice saying "no," take a self-defense course, or practice sustaining plank pose.

Anahata: Heart

This chakra resides in the heart and influences love, acceptance, self-compassion, and forgiveness. It involves our ability to keep an open heart, make connections, and balance self-care with care for others. It reminds us that cultivating loving relationships is an important part of the human journey. This area of the heart correlates to the element of air.

When this chakra is balanced we might feel a greater sense of love, joy, and gratitude. When this wheel is out of balance, we might experience isolation, bitterness, or lack of relatedness and empathy.

ONE DEGREE SHIFT INQUIRY:
Loving Fully

- How loving do you feel?
- Do you easily let love *in*?
- Do you allow yourself to give love?

If your answer to any of these questions is "no," your fourth chakra might be calling you. What might be a one degree shift that you could put yourself in to feel more balanced? For example, you might write a love letter to yourself, spend more time with people you care about, or practice supported bridge pose or other heart-opening postures.

Vishuddha: Expression

This chakra resides at the throat and influences communication, expression, and speaking truth. It involves our ability to listen, speak with intent, and connect to the ways that we vocalize our passions with the world. This center reminds us to use our voice to uplift and inspire and to speak the truth, and that our words hold power. This area of the throat correlates to the element ether.

When this chakra is balanced we feel free to communicate; our words are truthful and are used responsibly. When this wheel is out of balance, we may experience an uneasiness of speaking or a resistance about speaking up for oneself.

ONE DEGREE SHIFT INQUIRY:
Your Voice Matters

• Do you feel expressed?
• Do you feel your voice matters?

If your answer to either of these questions is "no," your fifth chakra might be calling you. What might be a one degree shift that you could put yourself in to feel more balanced? For example, you might speak a truth that you haven't yet, or take a public speaking or singing class, or practice postures to open the throat, like supported fish pose.

Ajna: Insight

This chakra resides right above the center of the eyebrows, and influences our feelings regarding intuition, perception, and reflection. This center reminds us that if we ignore the guidance of our inner knowing, we might end up regretting some of our choices. This area of intuition correlates to the element of light.

When this chakra is in balance we trust our intuition, are more discerning with what is true and real, and are open to receiving wisdom. When this wheel is out of balance, there might be an experience of not trusting your intuition, never taking personal alone time, and difficulty being aware of the gremlins.

ONE DEGREE SHIFT INQUIRY:
Trust Your Intuition

• Do you feel connected to an inner knowing?
• Do you trust your intuition?

If your answer to either of these questions is "no," your sixth chakra might be calling you. What might be a one degree shift that you could put yourself in to feel more balanced? For example, you might spend time journaling and reflecting, doing a yoga class with a softer gaze or in dim light to amplify your other senses, or practice child pose.

Sahasrara: Connection

This chakra resides at the crown of the head and influences feelings of connection to others, being a part of something greater. It invites us to live mindfully throughout our daily interactions with ourselves, others, and community/nature. This area of the head correlates to thought vibration.

When this chakra is balanced we are more able to trust life. When this wheel is out of balance we experience being overly individualistic, a poor relationship with the natural world, and confusion.

ONE DEGREE SHIFT INQUIRY:
Embracing the Mystery

• Do you feel connected to something greater than yourself?
• Do you feel at ease in the mystery of life?

If your answer to either of these questions is "no," your seventh chakra might be calling you. What might be a one degree shift that you could put yourself in to feel more balanced? For example, you might spend time volunteering, meditating, or practicing *savasana* (corpse pose).

ONE DEGREE SHIFT INQUIRY:
Creating a Hierarchy of Little c's

Make a list of all of the little c's that are getting your attention. You could review each chapter and see if a little c is trying to get your attention, or maybe there are other little c's that come to mind from the chakra inquiry.

You may have a very long list of little c's trying to get your attention. You get to decide which of these little c's holds more value or importance. And you may find that not every little c is of equal value, because there will be little c's that you care more about in this moment. You can always come back to the others at a later time. Again, it's not about doing everything at once—small shifts, big changes. Over time, you can go through your list, create small one degree shift inquiries for each, or see how they shift in priority based on what you've already worked on.

Once you have made your list, number them in the order that you would like to address them, with number one being the most important. Now, look at each little c in order, and ask yourself, "What is one small shift I could do in order to answer this calling?"

Number	Little c Calling	A Shift That Answers the Calling

The Relationship Between Big C and Little c's

Now that you have your life purpose statement to work with and a list of little c's, the next step is to see how they yoke together. Look at your list of little c's again and see which ones can support you in living out your Big C. Your little c's do not always need to support your Big C, yet in some instances they can and will. You can also look at it the other way: How can you live out your Big C, while taking action steps for the little c's that are important to you? For example, if you have a little c to start a business, and your Big C is to live a mindful life, you might ask yourself how you can create a business that is mindful of the impact it has on the planet.

Once you claim your Big C, you are invited to show up to it and actually take a stand by taking actions with your little c's. For example, if your life purpose is to share peace, then how you show up in your relationship, how you treat your family and friends, and how you engage at work are opportunities to live your Big C. Ask yourself, are you peaceful at work but showing up differently at your mom's house? If so, listen for the little c's that can help you live in alignment with your Big C. For example, you might recognize a little c to practice conscious communication with your mother so you can be more peaceful—your Big C.

I adopted my Big C, my life purpose, after studying with one of my teachers, Patrick Ryan. He taught me the phrase that I base my life purpose on, which is to be used well. By this I mean that I want to contribute to the world in a life-affirming way for the sake of truth, possibility, integrity, and love. All the choices I make are an opportunity to align with my life purpose. So when I wonder which way I should go or what I should do, I can ask, "Does this align with my Big C?" One of my little c's is sharing how to live yoga, and not just do yoga. I get to live my Big C and my little c with my daily work teaching, and by writing this book.

Yet "being used well" does not only happen at work—I try to live my Big C as often as I can, no matter what I am doing. I can be "used well" by smiling at a stranger, or helping someone in need, or being a good friend and listening when someone I love is having a hard day. I often check in at the end of the day and reflect on my ability to live out my life purpose that day. In an honest assessment, some days I feel like I am living my life purpose, and other days, not so much. Even on the days I don't feel totally aligned, I know that I am learning and have the opportunity to try again.

It's also perfectly okay if your Big C and little c's do not line up all the time. There are little c's that may call you—like singing at an open mic or burning all of your journals—that don't necessarily support your Big C. You are learning about life; there are things that may call you that you reflect on later and realize it was not for the sake of your Big C, or may not have been in alignment with your empowered self, and it still provides opportunities for growth.

ONE DEGREE SHIFT INQUIRY:
Relating Your Big C and Little c's

- What little c's have the most heart and meaning for you right now?
- How can your life purpose statement (Big C) support your little c's?

Gifts and Talents Can Make a Little c a Reality

Take a moment and reflect on your natural gifts, strengths, and/or talents that can support you living your little c's and your Big C. They can be used as leverage: they are your secret weapon that you can use to your advantage to bring your little c's to fruition.

Too often we forget to appreciate our unique contributions. Your gremlins may block you from seeing your talents in their most positive form, and only allow you to view them as burdens or drawbacks. The truth is, a gift or talent or strength can be both: it's up to you to decide how you want to use them and what you want to focus on.

Your talents, gifts, and strengths also offer clues to how your little c's will align with your Big C, or how your Big C will support the ways you live out your little c's.

ONE DEGREE SHIFT INQUIRY:
Gifts and Talents

- What are some of your gifts?
- What are some of your strengths?
- What are some of your talents?
- What comes naturally to you?
- What do you love to do? How does this positively impact your life and those around you?
- How have you been sharing these gifts, strengths, and talents?
- How could you share them more to support the little c that has the most heart and meaning for you?
- What do you do to strengthen these qualities even more?

How Serious Are You?

When we all start to live with purpose, we can recognize that we are all yoked together and that our choices impact one another. Your Big C is really a part of karma yoga, the yoga of action and service. So all of this work you've done to find your Big C is not just for you to ride the waves more easily: it is so you can also inspire, uplift, and support others. Remember, the boat isn't going anywhere until we are all on it.

You don't have to become the next Mother Teresa, and your Big C, little c's, and all your one degree shifts can still lead to big changes for the whole. When you begin to examine the way you show up in your life and choose to get in touch with your inner compass, you can guide yourself in a totally new direction—and inspire others to do the same. Together, we are evolving into our next perfection. So once you feel connected to your Big C, it is worthwhile to contemplate how connected you really are to this calling. As my teacher Lonny Jarrett once asked, "Are you serious, or are you deadly serious?"

How often do you start a new year with a list of resolutions, only to find a few weeks later that you have returned to your old behaviors? You're certainly not alone. So think of a moment you've tried to make a change. What would it take for you to become deadly serious about committing to that change? How much more successful could you be in living your life purpose?

For me, becoming deadly serious means paying extra attention to my behaviors, my choices, my "for the sake of." When we become deadly serious about our callings, we are recruiting our most aligned self to engage with life, which gives us even more energy to face some of the most intense gremlins. Being deadly serious calls me to sit in the fire, and to a level of resiliency deep within me to make a commitment to what I want to shift.

I imagine that most of us long for a more cooperative, kinder world. The lessons of this book were created to support you to begin doing your inner work, to make shifts in your life, and to go deep. And if the work is only about *you*, then in some ways you are missing out on the full potential of living yoga. In truth, our purpose always serves more than ourselves. Saying yes to your Big C and little c's is not just about *you*—it's about all of us. Because whether we like it or not, we are in this grand experiment of life together.

ONE DEGREE SHIFT INQUIRY:
Bringing Your Purpose to the World

For the sake of living into the Big C and little c's that are of high value to you, you are invited to practice putting yourself into a living *sadhana*. This exercise will span twenty-eight days because I always look to nature for inspiration, and want to align with the intelligence of life itself; in this case, the cycles of the moon.

First, ask yourself:

• How can I live my life purpose? What specific experiment can I put myself in to live my purpose over the next twenty-eight days? Write out your intended skillful action. If you were going to give someone else this description they would know exactly what it is you are planning on doing for this living sadhana.

• Set a start date for when you will begin and how much time you will dedicate to this practice each day.

• What is my Gremlin Action Plan that would support me during this experiment?

• What positive impact could my life purpose have on myself and others during this experiment?

Then, for the next twenty-eight days, you're going to move out of the philosophical part of living yoga, and begin your transformation. There's a big difference between philosophy and transformation: philosophy is a good idea, transformation is doing something about it. Every day offers the opportunity for you to practice living into your life's purpose in some tangible way. And every day will present an opportunity to ride the waves that may come up, or allow you to face your gremlins. The practice is to stay committed to your callings even if it becomes difficult, because most likely they have heart and meaning for you. That's living yoga.

On the twenty-ninth day, celebrate your willingness to live your callings. You could invite three of your closest friends to tell them about your experience and share what you learned. Treat yourself to something you have been longing to do, like a massage, a dance party, a special meal, etc. (it does not need to cost money). Treat yourself to a day of self-care, journaling, or a bath. Or invite your *kula* and have a party to celebrate the practice of practice!

Every cell in the body has a life purpose, a dharma.
You are a cell in the universe.
You are here to add your precious offering to the collective.
Like an unsung note,
it's time to sing, to share your voice.
What do you care enough about to bind yourself to it?
When each one of us says yes to our calling,
we've got the world covered.

—————⋄—————

II

Begin Again

We may not be able to undo the past.
But we can reset our choices today that will impact our tomorrow.
We can reset how we tend to our wounds.
We can reset our beliefs about our future.
We can reset the words we choose to use.
We can reset our careers.
We can reset our relationships.
We can reset how we treat our bodies.
We can reset how we view others.
We can reset how we treat each other.
We can reset whenever we want.
We can reset now.

One of the most important mantras I have ever learned is just two simple words: begin again. To me, these words offer endless opportunities, and in many ways, explain why yoga has endured. It is a wisdom and depth practice that you can return to and gain new insights wherever you are on the journey of life.

If you subscribe to the belief that life is a process, a blossoming and unfolding—you will begin to see that there is no "end of the road," and rather there is always more to experience. Experience has a beginning, a middle, and an end, only to begin again. At some point you start to look forward to the cycles, the rhythms, and see them all as another chance to live yoga. Every breath of every moment of every day is an opportunity to practice, to engage, to participate: to learn to sit in the fire, to live with our highest integrity and authenticity, to take responsibility for our actions, to be supportive of others, or to be daring enough to ask for help, to pause, to compost your old story into fuel to create a new story, to trust the mystery of life, to soften and surrender, and to listen for the calling that is knocking at your heart and live out your life purpose. Life truly is a grand experiment.

By living yoga, every day offers the opportunity to ask yourself, "How do I want to show up today?" And with that invitation comes the ability to be a more empowered version of yourself, just by making one small shift. Every day presents the chance to get back on the boat, or practice riding the waves. You can let go of who you were, and choose who you want to be and where you want to go. Let go of the "I should have" or "I can't believe I didn't," and allow yourself to wake up to the possibilities that you've discovered in these inquiries.

And even though you are well on your way to charting a new course, be kind when you don't show up as your most empowered self. Sometimes life gets in the way. Yet no matter how big the waves get, if you get knocked down, if you seem like you are going in an unexpected direction—you can always, always, always begin again. You can adjust, modify, or even make a different one degree shift. Yoga is about skillfully participating and engaging—not sitting on the shore. With a gentle nudge, get yourself back out there and begin again.

The practice of beginning again is a sacred practice in itself. The inquiries and experiments you've put yourself in are not meant to be a "one and done" experience. My hope is that this book provides a place that you can return to again and again, whenever the waves feel too big or you are not sure which way to go. You could pick any inquiry in this book and it could be your practice for a week, a year, or even a lifetime. Or, you can reexamine a particular tool, inquiry, or experiment to help you learn how to fully savor the precious gift of life—to see its inherent beauty. Maybe you skipped over some, didn't feel you were ready, or resistance or a gremlin took over. As you continue to circle back, you will feel the richness and the depth that each one can offer, to keep evolving into the next perfection of yourself. And in this way, these inquiries, and living yoga, are a lifelong practice.

ONE DEGREE SHIFT INQUIRY:
Change Your Questions, Change Your Life

The inquiries you've put yourself into have put you on a whole new course. With the mind-set of "begin again," what if you changed the questions slightly? Each time we refine the questions we ask we change the answers we find.

So what's trying to get your attention now?

- Instead of "What am I seeking," you could ask, "What am I finding?"
- What isn't working vs. what is working?
- How are my gremlins holding me back vs. how have my gremlins transformed?

At some point you might realize you don't need
to save the world to save the world.
You will understand the power in small shifts.
You will come to understand that moments are
precious and life is sacred.
You will appreciate the three amazing friends you have rather
than the thousands of "friends" you have.
You will realize that we are drops from the same
ocean—we are in this together.
You will stop listening so tightly to "teachers" and
trust the teacher inside.
You will realize that everyone is fighting a battle and not
everyone's battle needs to be your battle.
You will realize some people choose to stay angry and some people
use their anger as fuel for change.
You will see what is trendy and what you are supposed to care
about, and you will feel comfort in what you actually care about.
You will realize that there really are wonderful people on the
planet, and a handful of incredibly hurt and misguided souls
making a lot of noise.
You will appreciate the times of excitement, enthusiasm, and
passion, and also the moments of softness, gentleness, and rest.
You will judge less and love more—not because you have been

told you should, but because you really, finally get it—
love is the answer.
You will realize that forgiveness is a gift to yourself and that
boundaries can be an act of love.
You will speak up when it matters and listen even more.
You will trust life, because you have been carried by the current
enough times that you actually trust life.
May we all celebrate the gift of life today.
May we walk a little softer, speak a little kinder,
and love a little harder.